Going to live in

Australia

Going to live in
Australia

Your Practical Guide to living and working in Oz

Mary Neilson & Mathew Collins

howtobooks

First published by
How To Books Ltd
Spring Hill House, Spring Hill Road, Begbroke,
Oxford OX5 1RX, United Kingdom.
Tel: (01865) 375794. Fax: (01865) 379162.
info@howtobooks.co.uk
www.howtobooks.co.uk

Reprinted 2004
Reprinted 2005
Second edition 2008

British Library Cataloguing in Publication Data
A catalogue record for this book is available from the British Library

ISBN 978 1 84528 261 5

Illustrations by Nickie Averill
Cover design by Baseline Arts Ltd, Oxford
Produced for How To Books by Deer Park Productions, Tavistock, Devon
Typeset by PDQ Typesetting, Newcastle-under-Lyme, Staffs.
Printed and bound by Cromwell Press, Trowbridge, Wiltshire

NOTE: The material contained in this book is set out in good faith for
general guidance and no liability can be accepted
for loss or expense incurred as a result of relying in particular circumstances
on statements made in the book. The laws and regulations are complex and
liable to change, and readers should check the current position with the
relevant authorities before making personal arrangements.

Contents

Preface

In today's electronic world and marketplace, global traveller and businesses are driving and increasing the demand of those who want to live in a different location. The advent of e-mail and the Internet is contributing to the necessity for accurate immigration information.

Australia, one of the most multicultural countries in the world, is extremely popular with holidaymakers and others wanting a complete change of lifestyle. This unique environment is home to people from most of the world's nations, and is now a rich and fascinating potpourri of cultural diversity. Australia's changing and developing society and dynamic economy are fuelled by the constant review and updating of immigration policies. These policies embrace all facets of life, including business, education and the family. We have written this book to simplify the above and assist you in starting a new life in Australia – possibly the biggest change you and your family will undertake in life.

Immigration, like most government policies and laws, is a complex subject to tackle. Mathew Collins, having practised as an immigration consultant for ten years, is very experienced at providing the answers to the most common questions that people ask: 'How do I migrate to Australia?', 'How long does it take?', 'How much does it cost?' and 'Am I likely to succeed?' He has clearly identified current Australian immigration policies and procedures to help you to understand them, and any implications they have for you.

Using her knowledge and research skills as a well-travelled writer, parent, business woman and Antipodean, Mary Neilson has presented a broad, yet detailed outline of the mechanics of making the move. The history of this magnificent country, the most important aspects to consider when making your decision and essential information on the law, customs and lifestyle of Australia are all covered. Moving, finding a home, settling your family and healthcare are all discussed with useful contact details in each section. Even how to move your pets is included.

This book discusses staying in Australia temporarily and permanently, family categories, employer-sponsored categories, setting up business, business skills and investment categories. We have included as many useful contacts as possible for up-to-date information and documentation for your application. We envisage that your copy of *Going to Live in Australia* will become an invaluable and 'dog-eared' guide which will help you and your family to adapt readily to a new and exciting way of life in a wonderful country.

After reading this book, we hope you will be confident enough to either handle your own case or tell your visa consultant what you hope to accomplish.

Good luck!

Mary Neilson
Mathew Collins

A map of Australia.

Part One
Australia past and present

1

Introducing Australia

HISTORY AND BACKGROUND

About 50 million years ago, as dinosaurs were disappearing from Earth, Australia was formed when a piece of land broke away from Gondwanaland, the large land mass that included Africa, South America and India. Today, huge parts of the Australian landscape show movements in the Earth that occurred more than 1,000 million years ago. In the central plateau, which covers half of the continent and includes the Kimberly and Hamersley ranges, the Great Sandy, Great Victoria and Gibson Deserts, rocks with the embedded remains of organisms dating back 3,500 million years, have been found. Some of man's oldest tools, a dinosaur's footprint, and evidence of coral reefs in a sea where landlocked ocean fish have adapted to fresh water, have also been discovered. The world's only egg-laying mammals, the platypus and echidna and over 120 different species of marsupials (the red kangaroo, koala and tiny desert mice) are synonymous with Australia and have developed in extraordinary ways in this isolated, unique land.

As long ago as 8,000 BC, Aboriginal hunters, who understood intimately the vagaries of the land and climate, invented the returning boomerang to kill the creatures they stalked. Sometimes they patiently tracked their prey for days while the women fished and gathered food. Clans of ten to 50 maintained nature's balance and took only what was needed to feed themselves. Practising conservation in this way, they ensured there was always adequate food for their people. The term 'Dreamtime' embraces the Aboriginal cultural heritage and defines traditional thought and practice. Spirits and legends as depicted in rock drawings, paintings, dances and songs, describe the close link between the land and its people. As with other indigenous groups, to take land from an Aborigine is to take his life, both spiritually and literally. In the 1770s the estimated Aboriginal population was more than three hundred thousand. The first settlers regarded the 500 different and complex Aboriginal languages as 'babble' and as a consequence only 30 dialects are spoken today. A culture that was 50,000 years old was ill-prepared for the white man's arrival, the subsequent land grabbing and the onslaught of savagery and foreign diseases.

In 1290, Marco Polo speculated about a land rich in gold and shells, lying south of Java, as did the Greeks, Arabs, and Portuguese, whose maps recorded that they were familiar with the eastern half of Australia. The Portuguese explorer, Queiros, named the island of Vanuatu, 'Australia del Espiritu Santo', mistakenly thinking it was the Australian continent. It is possible that Chinese sandalwood cutters from Timor arrived in the thirteenth and fourteenth centuries, and in support of that theory, a small statuette from the Ming Dynasty was unearthed in Darwin in 1879.

A Dutchman, Willem Janz, made Australia's first known landing in 1606 and Abel Tasman followed in 1642 with a sighting of the west coast of Tasmania, which he called 'Van Dieman's Land' or 'New Holland'.

William Dampier, while looking for new trade routes to the Pacific, was the first Englishman to set foot on the continent in 1688. Then, Captain James Cook anchored in Botany Bay for a week on 28 April 1770. Later, sailing north, Cook hoisted the British flag on Possession Island on 22 August, naming the eastern side of the continent 'New South Wales'. Originally sent by the Royal Society to observe the transit of Venus, Cook and his naturalist, Joseph Banks, thrilled English society with drawings and tales of the strange animals, plants and 'noble savages' found on this new land.

After their losses in the American War of Independence, the British needed another place to send the unwanted dregs of society – drunks, petty thieves and criminals. And on 26 January 1788 the first fleet of eleven ships carrying 1,000 passengers – three-quarters of them convicts – arrived at Port Jackson and raised the British flag to proclaim the new nation. The Sydney Opera House now overlooks this cove. A second coastal penal settlement was established in Tasmania in 1825. From the first colony, exploration and settlement spread. At the same time, the British Government was giving away free land in order to encourage people to move away from the overcrowded shores of Britain to an apparently empty land in Australia.

Between 1840 and 1869 the transportation of convicts gradually stopped, and in 1860 the continent was divided into five separate colonies. Tensions increased between Europeans and Aborigines, squatters (rich officers and free – not convict – settlers who 'squatted' or laid claim to large tracts of land for merino sheep stations), and farmers (Australian-born or free settlers), often creating a hostile environment. The new arrivals, claiming possession of land that they assumed was uninhabited, were not welcomed by Aborigines. Settlers started to greatly outnumber the convict population, and settlements spread to South Australia in 1837. Victoria sprang up in 1851, Queensland in 1859, and the Swan River Colony, which had been established in 1827, became self-governing in 1890. The Commonwealth of Australia was formed in 1901 through the proclamation of the Constitution for the Federation of Six States. The original fathers at the forefront of this new nation, wanting to avoid the pitfalls of their homelands, had progressive ideas about the rights of man, democratic procedures and the value of a secret ballot. Since 1901, the constitutional ties with Britain have slowly loosened.

EUREKA! GOLD...

Much of Australia is a plateau, bounded by four seas and three oceans, with an average elevation of three hundred and thirty metres, the lowest of the world's continents. Early exploration of Australia progressed slowly because of the inhospitable terrain and climate of the large continent. The barrier of the Blue Mountains to the west of Sydney and the difficult nature of the Australian bush were other reasons for the slow pace of development.

The discovery of gold at Bathurst, by Edward Hargraves in May 1851, put Australia firmly on the map. Eager prospectors worldwide and from other colonies, such as Victoria, where the population rapidly declined, rushed to Bathurst. This was the first of many subsequent gold finds which attracted a flood of migrants to the Australian shores. Miners, who came initially for gold, remained as settlers and contributed their skills to the new land. This rapid economic growth made it possible for Australia to become relatively independent of Britain.

Irish immigrants or runaway convicts, often those of strong Republican sentiments who rebelled against Protestant landlords and those in authority, usually the British, were known as 'bush-rangers'. Ned Kelly was one of these outlaws who, even though he killed three policemen, is today part of Australian folklore. Wimbledon tennis champion Pat Cash's ancestor was another renowned colonial highwayman, and the restaurant chain Cobb and Co. is named after the stagecoaches that carried gold or lone travellers, 'rich pickings' for opportunistic robbers.

PEACE, PROSPERITY AND CHANGE IN THE 1900s

By 1880, Australia's population was two million, increasing to six million by the end of the First World War. The number of Australians employed in the manufacturing industry increased steadily after the 1900s and many women who had worked in traditional men's jobs during the war continued to work during peacetime.

The establishment of a capital city for the country became a priority. Sydney and Melbourne bitterly contested the right to be the designated capital. The Government compromised in 1913 by naming Canberra, a new Territory on the Monaro Tablelands, which lay between the two cities, as head of the nation.

The output of primary industries, such as wheat and wool, continued to grow, although the percentage of rural sector workers started to decline. After the Second World War, European immigration was encouraged and the nation enjoyed a boom period of rapid industrialisation. In 1948, with American finance and migrant labour, Australia's first car manufacturing plant, General Motors, started producing the Holden saloon.

The economy developed strongly in the 1950s, with the opening up of mining resources and major nation-building projects such as the huge hydroelectricity generator project in the Snowy Mountains. A prosperous society meant that everyone benefited, suburban property ownership increased and the Government consolidated its political stability.

The influx of immigrants between 1945 and 1965 increased the population from seven million to eleven million and dramatically changed the cultural, culinary and psychological face of Australia. During this period of rapid population growth, the Australian Government tried to prevent the immigration of Asian and Pacific Islander people by passing the Immigration Restriction Bill, more commonly known as the 'White Australian Policy'. This Bill was later revoked. Until recently, Australian immigration policies encouraged British applications for permanent residency and citizenship and, as a consequence, most of the United Kingdom's population seems to have at least one relative living in Australia.

In the 60s, as with the rest of the Western world, Australia's society changed because of increasing ethnic diversity, Britain's declining influence as a world power and the increasing domination of the United States, especially during the Vietnam War. The growth of the 'Baby Boomers' impacted the nation's focus, causing significant economic, political and social change.

The long post-war domination of the national political scene by the National Party finished in 1972 when the Labor Party was elected to power. The following three years saw subsequent reforms and major legislative changes in education, health, social security, foreign affairs and industrial relations. However, in 1975 a constitutional crisis resulted in the Prime Minister, Gough Whitlam, being dismissed by the Governor General and the subsequent defeat of the Labor Party in the following election. The National Party dominated the political scene until 1983 when Labor returned to office. The previous Coalition Government, led by John Howard, was defeated late in 2007 by Kevin Rudd leading the Labor Party. The Labor Party is the opposition. Other mainstream political parties are the Australian Democrats, the Australian Greens, a rising political force, and a Christian party, Family First.

2

Australia Today

Australia in the twenty-first century is the world's sixth largest nation after Russia, Canada, China, the United States of America and Brazil and, although lacking in height, the enormous variety of this magnificent land mass more than compensates with spectacular sights, such as the giant monolith Uluru – more commonly known as Ayers Rock – the Great Barrier Reef and the vast Australian outback. These wonders of nature represent a huge industry and attraction for tourists worldwide.

The 2006 United Nations Human Development Report, which ranks countries primarily on people's equality of life based on economic values, nominated Australia as third best place to live in the world, up one rank from the previous report. The current Economist Intelligence Unit's Survey based on climate, material wellbeing of the populace, family and community life, job security, political stability and freedom, designated Australia as the sixth best country in the world to live. Sydney, Melbourne, Perth, Adelaide and Brisbane are ranked in the top 30 of 200+ cities as best places to live.

The stars on the Australian flag designed in 1901 represent the Southern Cross and Australia's geographic position in the Southern Hemisphere, while the large Commonwealth star represents the federation of States and Territories. In 1984 'Advance Australia Fair' became the first official national anthem and the continent's population of over 20 million celebrates 'Australia Day' each year on 26 January.

The Australian Coat of Arms is a shield with badges of the Six States and features the national symbols of golden wattle, the kangaroo and the emu. Australia was the first country in the world to introduce banknotes made of polymer which are harder to counterfeit and last longer than the previous paper ones.

With a stable political environment and one of the world's most innovative, deregulated free market economies, Australia relies on service and leading-edge industries as well as its traditional role as a commodity exporter. An earlier A$2.9 billion, five-year programme called 'Backing Australia's Ability' provided funding to enhance innovative skills and develop new technology and the use of e-commerce to promote commercial success. More than 840 international companies have established their Asia Pacific headquarters in Australia to take advantage of the advanced communications infrastructure and wide range of native Asian language skills available. The latter is the result of Australia's planned 50-year post-war immigration policy, which has welcomed nearly six million migrants, including over 600,000 refugees. Assuming that current immigration policies continue, preliminary figures estimate that Australia's economy will benefit over the next ten years by the equivalent of A$30 billion at present rates. Research shows that only 18 months after settling into their new home, *recent skilled migrants' earnings are well above the national average weekly wage.* Immigration has created a diverse multicultural society with a huge impact on, and benefit to, all aspects of the Australian community. With a great climate, food, wine, friendly people, cosmopolitan and relaxed lifestyle, Australia is one of the world's most popular tourist destinations and a desirable place to live.

ABORIGINES

In 1901, the right to vote was denied Aborigines as they were considered a dying race. It was obvious by the 1930s that the indigenous people of Australia were not a dying race, and their political awareness developed until young activists in the 1960s demanded that racist and discriminatory legislation be abolished. In 1967, Australian citizens voted overwhelmingly during a national referendum to give the Federal Government the power to pass legislation on behalf of Australia's indigenous people. This showed an enormous amount of support throughout Australia for improving the living conditions of both the Aboriginal and Torres Strait Islander communities. A Department of Aboriginal Affairs was set up in 1972 and a new policy of self-determination allowed Aborigines to retain their cultural values and identity, and make decisions regarding their future. It also gave them the right to achieve social and economic equality alongside fellow Australians. In 1975, the Northern Territory Land Rights Act gave these ancient peoples the right to claim back their land. In 1988, Australia's bi-centenary of European settlement was marked by Aborigines with a massive land march called a Year of Mourning, which conversely, also celebrated their survival. The High Court in 1993 rejected the view that Australia was unoccupied when the first fleet of settlers arrived, and recognised the right of Aborigines to claim sections of unoccupied land throughout the country. The Federal Government in Canberra in the early 1990s agreed to 'hand-back' ceremonies of sites sacred to the Aborigine, such as Uluru (Ayers Rock) and Kakadu in the Northern Territory and the southern part of Jervis Bay in New South Wales. The Reconciliation Movement, which fostered events such as the People's Walk For Reconciliation across the Sydney Harbour Bridge on 28 May 2000, was formed to try and address some of the historical and painful issues from the past. There is still a long way to go as many States have yet to recognise Aboriginal land rights. Discrimination, unemployment and health are ongoing and huge concerns for Aborigines, even though their culture and traditions are recognised as a unique heritage synonymous with Australia.

FACTS AND FIGURES

- Population 21,701,488

- Land mass 7.69 square kilometres

◆ Coastline 8000 km

◆ **State/territory**

State/territory	population	capital
NSW	6,817,812	Sydney
Victoria	5,128,310	Melbourne
Queensland	4,091,546	Brisbane
Western Aust.	2,059,045	Perth
Southern Aust.	1,568,204	Adelaide
Tasmania	489,922	Hobart
Aust. Capital Territory	334,225	Canberra
Northern Territory	210,674	Darwin

◆ Net gain of 1 x international immigrant every three minutes

◆ Workforce approximately 10.5 million

◆ Average monthly mortgage: A$800–A$1200

◆ Average weekly rent: A$165–A$275

◆ Average weekly income: A$550

◆ Average weekly family income: A$1200

◆ Gross Domestic Product: A$720 billion

◆ Wine exports have doubled since 2000–1, making Australia one of the largest wine producers in the world. Approximately 800 million litres exported annually. It is feared the current drought will drastically affect this industry.

◆ Inflation rate: June 2007: 2.1%

◆ All registered motor vehicles: 13.5 million

◆ People with mobile phones: 18 million (est.)

- 10 per cent tax on goods and services (GST)

- National colours: green and gold

- Australia has three time zones:
  East: GMT + 10
  Central: GMT + 9.5
  West: GMT + 8

- Flight times from Sydney to Perth 5 hours; Adelaide to Darwin: 3 hours 40 minus

- 954 internet providers

- Households with internet access: 66%

- Adults accessing internet/yr: 85%

- Households with computers: 70%

- Items handled by postal service: 5.42 billion

- Overseas visitors: 7.5 million (est.)

- Lowest point: 15 metres below sea level (dry bed of Lake Eyre, South Australia)

- Highest point 2228 metres above sea level (Mt Kosciuszko, New South Wales)

GOVERNMENT

The Commonwealth of Australia is a constitutional monarchy, a federation and a parliamentary democracy. The Commonwealth of Australia was formed in 1901 as a result of an agreement between the six democratic, previously self-governing British colonies. Like the United States and unlike Britain, Australia has a written constitution, which defines foreign relations, trade defence and immigration. Protected by law, religious tolerance, freedom of association and speech are important aspects of this robust and pioneering democracy.

The Governor General is nominated by the Federal Government to represent the Queen as the Head of State. The British Crown in each State is represented by a Governor, now a largely symbolic role, as proved in the 1999 referendum when Australia nearly became a republic.

Australia's Federal Government, the Six States and the two self-governing Territories all share in the responsibility of governing the vast land area. There are three levels of government in Australia, with the upper house called the Senate, which acts mainly as a house of review. The referential voting system is compulsory and transparent, with the right to change government taken seriously by 90% of the population.

Australia's wealth, outward-looking policies and stability have made this country important in world events. It is a part of the Commonwealth of Nations, was a founding member of the United Nations and was instrumental in the founding of the Asia-Pacific Economic Cooperation forum (APEC).

The Federal Government

The Federal or Commonwealth Government is based on a popularly elected parliament, headed by the Prime Minister, the leader of the House of Representatives. The party with the majority vote holds the greatest number of seats in the

Lower House. Power is shared between a Federal Government and the Six States. The Australian Capital, Canberra and the Northern Territories self-govern.

The State and Territory Governments

The State and Territory Governments or Parliaments adhere to the national Constitution and are responsible for education, transport, health and law enforcement. They are generally led by a premier elected by the party holding power. Income tax is levied federally so revenue expenditure is usually an election issue.

There are eight administrative regions:

> States: Queensland (QLD), New South Wales (NSW), Victoria (VIC), Tasmania (TAS), South Australia (SA), Western Australia (WA)
> Territories: Northern Territory (NT), Australian Capital Territory (ACT).

The Australian Constitution created a federal legislature, the Parliament of the Commonwealth. Under the Constitution, the six colonies became States of the Commonwealth of Australia. Each state has its own constitution so that Australia has seven sovereign Parliaments, none of which can encroach on the functions of any other. The High Court of Australia arbitrates on any disputes which arise between the Commonwealth and the States, or among the States, concerning their respective functions.

The Commonwealth Parliament can propose changes to the Constitution. To become effective, the proposals must be put to a referendum of all Australians of voting age, and most receive a 'double majority':

◆ a majority of all votes, and
◆ a majority of votes in a majority of States.

All States elect 12 Senators, regardless of population. This ensures a fair representation no matter the size of the State.

Local government
Local government receives funding from rates and higher government and is responsible for the operation of transport and energy enterprises. Other responsibilities may include town planning, building codes, local roads, effluent and water services and community facilities.

Useful websites for further information:

> *www.fed.gov.au* (for information and services)
> *www.cultureandrecreation.gov.au* (for information on culture and recreation)
> *http://en.wikipedia.org/wiki/government_of_australia*

THE LEGAL SYSTEM

Australian law and customs
In a tolerant society where many people of different cultures and backgrounds live, knowing and understanding the customs and laws of that country help one to adapt and settle. Migrants to Australia are encouraged to retain and share their traditions and culture while observing their new country's customs and laws. A

commitment to living in Australia means that the rights of others to observe their customs and traditions are equally respected. The following should be noted:

- Equality in Australia means that everyone has the right to be treated the same as anyone else regardless of race, country of origin, sex, marital status, pregnancy, political and religious belief. This applies to employment, accommodation, purchase of goods and use of services like banks, hotels and doctors. Men and women are equal by law.

- Violence in any place including the home and within marriage is illegal and unacceptable in Australia. The law also protects children from violence and abuse both at home and at school.

- Animals and birds may not be mistreated with cruelty and neglect, or the perpetrators may be imprisoned or fined. Each State has local laws on the domestic animals that can be kept and dogs are usually required to be registered.

- Smoking is generally prohibited in workplaces, and most States also prohibit smoking in restaurants and shopping centres. A sign will usually indicate where smoking is prohibited, but it is appreciated if one enquires where the smoking areas are before lighting up. Selling or supplying cigarettes or tobacco to anyone less than 18 years, by law a minor, is prohibited in most Australian States and Territories.

- Narcotic drugs are prohibited in Australia and the penalties for importation and use are severe and usually result in imprisonment. Be wary about any stranger who may ask you to carry anything for them when you are travelling.

◆ Drinking and possessing alcohol in some public places is prohibited, as is the supply or sale of alcohol to a minor. The law allows minors to have alcohol in their possession only on a private property, which may be their home.

◆ Driving laws, particularly when driving after drinking and speeding, are very strict and can result in fines, imprisonment or the loss of your licence. The permitted levels of blood alcohol may vary throughout Australia. Everyone in a vehicle must use their seatbelts and children require an approved restraint. The police have to be contacted immediately if you are involved in a car accident.

◆ The environment is protected by laws that make it an offence to litter, create pollution, or dispose of waste. A clean environment and the legislation to support it are very important to Australians. Native plants, shellfish, animals and fish are protected and you will probably require a permit before you go fishing, shellfish gathering, hunting or collecting any wild plants. The National Parks are also very protected and you need to be familiar with the laws and restrictions before visiting them.

◆ Noise regulations vary between States and Territories and whether the area is zoned for residential, commercial or industrial use. Most people are tolerant of sporadic noise, but laws protect Australians from excessively loud, frequent or night-time noise and a complaint can be made to your local council, the police, and the State or Territory environment authority. Contact details will be in the front part of the phone directory.

♦ Free or subsidised legal advice provided by the Government or community includes legal aid, consumer affairs, anti-discrimination and the Ombudsman's offices. It is advisable to appoint a lawyer to oversee your affairs.

Part Two
Entry into Australia

3

Staying in Australia Temporarily

People holidaying in Australia must seek a visitor visa (tourist class) from the Australian High Commission. Australia offers visitors a visa that lasts three months or one that lasts for six months. If you are issued with a three-month visa you must enter within 12 months from the date of issue. However, if you receive a six-month visa then you may enter within four years from the date of issue, or before the passport expires, whichever occurs first. Australia has very strict rules on overstaying so it is vital that applicants do not fall into an overstay situation.

All people applying for a temporary residence visa must meet health and character criteria. In line with this, some applicants may need to undergo a medical and a chest X-ray before approval is given.

A person on a temporary residence visa will normally be allowed to travel out of and re-enter Australia for the duration of their visa. It is worth noting that people who stay in the country past the expiry of their visa seriously jeopardise their right to future visits or migration plans.

Australia offers a wide range of visa categories to enable you to stay in the country on a temporary basis. Over the 2006/2007 financial year more than 100,000 temporary visas were granted to overseas citizens.

Temporary residents with the right to work must pay taxes on any income earned in Australia. They will normally be prevented from claiming social welfare benefits or national public health cover unless they come from a country that has a reciprocal health care agreement with the Australian government.

THE WORKING HOLIDAY SCHEME

The Working Holiday Scheme encourages an international understanding between countries, it provides opportunities for young people to experience Australia through travel and holidaying and allows them limited work opportunities. Australia has reciprocal agreements with the following countries:

Belgium, Canada, Chile, Cyprus (Republic of), Denmark, Estonia, Finland, France, Germany, HKSAR*, Ireland (Republic of), Italy, Japan, Korea (Republic of), Netherlands, Norway, Sweden, Taiwan, Thailand, Turkey, the United Kingdom

---

*Hong Kong Special Administration Region of the People's Republic of China

The Working Holiday Scheme is available to those whose intentions are as follows:

- The main reason for travel to Australia is for a holiday, and that any work taken will be incidental to support themselves while holidaying.

- They will not enrol to study, apart from a short-term English language courses.

- They will leave Australia at the end of their authorised stay.

CATEGORIES FOR TEMPORARY IMMIGRATION

Investor Retirement category

Qualifying retirees may live in Australia for a period of four years. The requirements for this visa are that the main applicant must:

- be at least 55 years of age
- have no dependants other than a spouse or de facto partner
- meet the health and character requirements
- be sponsored by a State/Territory Government Agency.

You must also have minimum assets legally owned and acquired by you and your spouse (if applicable) which you are able to transfer to Australia, of:

- A$500,000 if you have indicated to your chosen State/Territory Agency that it is your intention to live in a regional/low growth area of Australia; or

- A$750,000 if you have indicated to your chosen State/ Territory agency that you do not intend to live in a regional/low growth area of Australia

In addition, you must also be in a position to show the following:

- that you have an annual net income stream (for instance pension) which you and your spouse can access of A$50,000 if it is your intention to live in a regional/low-growth area of Australia

- that you have an annual net income stream (for instance pension) which you and your spouse have access to of A$65,000 if it is not your intention to live in a regional/low-growth area of Australia.

You are required to be in a position to make a designated investment of:

- A$500,000 in your own or your spouse's name in the State/Territory from which you have gained sponsorship, if you have advised your sponsoring State/ Territory agency that you intend to live in a regional area of Australia; or

- A$750,000 in your own or your spouse's name in the State/Territory from which you have gained sponsorship, if you have advised your sponsoring State/ Territory agency that you intend to live in a non-regional area of Australia

These assets must have been owned by you for a period of at least two years, unless these are related to pensions or inheritance. Additionally you must show evidence that you have purchased for yourself, and your spouse, if applicable, a private health insurance package which meets Australian Department of Health and Ageing (DHA) requirements for the full term of your intended stay in Australia. Retirement visas now include limited work rights which will allow the holder to work for a maximum of 20 hours per week.

Please be advised that New South Wales is not currently offering sponsorship for this visa category.

Should you wish to extend your stay at the end of the initial four-year period of this visa you will be required to show evidence that you meet the following criteria:

- be at least 55 years of age
- have no dependants other than a spouse or de facto partner
- meet the health and character requirements
- be sponsored by a State/Territory Government agency.

You must be able to make a designated investment of:

- A$250,000 if you have indicated to your chosen State/Territory Agency that it is your intention to live in a regional/low-growth area of Australia; or

- A$500,000 if you have indicated to your chosen State/Territory Agency that you do not intend to live in a regional/low-growth area of Australia.

In addition, you must also be in a position to show the following:

♦ that you have an annual net income stream (for instance pension) which you and your spouse can access of A$50,000 if it is your intention to live in a regional/low-growth area of Australia

♦ that you have an annual net income stream (for instance pension) which you and your spouse have access to of A$65,000 if it is not your intention to live in a regional/low-growth area of Australia.

You are further required to show evidence that you, and your spouse, if applicable, have held private health insurance which meets the requirements of the Department of Health and Ageing (DHA) for the term of your original visa and continue to hold this.

Additionally you are required to provide evidence that you are:

♦ of good character

♦ meet health requirements (at this time streamlined health criteria will apply and the examinations you undergo will be restricted to examinations for conditions considered as public health risks by Australia).

Designated investments are offered by the State and Territory Treasury Corporations as:

♦ primary issue Government securities with a maturity of no less than that four years from the date of purchase

◆ limited to investments detailed for the Investor Retirement Visa with interest paid at six-monthly intervals

◆ are non-transferrable and non-redeemable.

Repayment of your initial investment on maturity is guaranteed by the State or Territory Government.

The following table shows details of those postcodes which are deemed to be regional/low-growth areas of Australia.

Regional Australia/low population-growth metropolitan areas

	Postcodes inclusive
New South Wales except Sydney, Newcastle, the Central Coast and Wollongong	2311 to 2312
	2328 to 2411
	2420 to 2490
	2536 to 2551
	2575 to 2594
	2618 to 2739
	2787 to 2898
Queensland except the greater Brisbane area and the Gold Coast	4124 to 4125
	4133
	4211
	4270 to 4272
	4275
	4280
	4285
	4287
	4307 to 4499
	4515
	4517 to 4519
	4522 to 4899

Victoria except Melbourne Metropolitan Area	3211 to 3334
	3340 to 3424
	3430 to 3649
	3658 to 3749
	3753
	3756
	3758
	3762
	3764
	3778 to 3781
	3783
	3797
	3799
	3810 to 3909
	3921 to 3925
	3945 to 3974
	3979
	3981 to 3996
Western Australia except Perth and surrounding areas	6041 to 6044
	6083 to 6084
	6121 to 6126
	6200 to 6799
South Australia	Entire State
Tasmania	Entire State
Northern Territory	Entire Territory

Emergency category

Allows applicants who have applied for a temporary residency visa, but are awaiting the approval on the health and character criteria, the right to travel to Australia if they can demonstrate an urgent need to do so.

Confirmatory category

Approves the stay of people who have entered Australia on an emergency visa once their outstanding health and character checks have been met.

Exchange category

Allows citizens from countries that have reciprocal arrangements to enter Australia.

Foreign Government Agency category

Employees of foreign governments which have no official status, or those officials who do not have diplomatic or official status, have the right to stay in Australia on the basis of carrying out official business.

Special Program

Allows Churchill fellows or other approved community based non-commercial programmes' members the chance to enter Australia to develop international relations.

Visiting Academic category

People who have been invited by an Australian research or tertiary institute may travel to Australia to observe and participate (without payment) in projects.

Entertainment category

Grants entry for performers and their supporters who will be involved with the Australian entertainment industry.

Sport category

Allows sportspeople, sporting officials and support staff to engage in competitions and training in Australia.

Media and Film category

Professional media and support staff may seek entry under this category.

Public Lecturer category

This enables professional lectures and recognised experts

to take up invitations to make public presentations.

Family Relationship category

This provides the opportunity of an extended holiday for young people under the age of 18 to stay with relatives or close family friends in Australia.

Domestic Worker/Diplomatic or Consular category

Allows entry for domestic workers and official staff in Australia. The application must be supported by the Australian Department of Foreign Affairs and Trade.

Religious Worker category

Allows religious and evangelical workers to serve the spiritual needs of their faith in Australia.

Supported Dependant (of an Australian or New Zealand citizen) category

Allows for dependent family unit members of Australian citizens, permanent residents and eligible New Zealand citizens temporary residence in Australia.

Expatriate category

Gives the right of temporary residence to the dependants of expatriate employees stationed in isolated locations in Papua New Guinea, the South Pacific and South East Asia.

Diplomatic category

Gives approval for diplomats, consular officials and employees and certain members of specialist United Nations agencies temporary entry into Australia.

4

Staying in Australia Permanently

In the post-Second World War era Australia set up a large-scale migration programme in agreement with the British, other European countries and the International Refugee Organisation to encourage migration, especially from war-torn Europe.

Since this time the migration programme has undergone many changes, revisions and updates to take into account the changing needs of the Australian economy and society. This migration programme has seen approximately 6 million people settle in Australia and the population rise from 7 million to 20 million. Successive governments have modified and developed policy around the needs of the country, the people and the economy.

Today Australia is one of the few countries in the world to run a permanent migration programme to actively encourage potential migrants to settle in the country. The policy is non-discriminatory and means that anyone from any country can apply to migrate regardless of their gender, ethnic origin or religion.

In broad terms the immigration programme can be split into the following categories.

MIGRATION PROGRAMME

Family stream
Allows people with family links to Australian citizens or permanent residence the right to live and work in Australia.

Skilled stream
Seeks to bring in people with business, work skills or other special talents that would be of benefit to Australia's economic growth.

The government hopes to attract in excess of 100,000 immigrants for 2007/2008 places on the permanent migration programme, with roughly half going to people with family links in Australia. The remainder will possess business or professional skills and abilities. There is also a humanitarian programme for refugees and displaced people who have suffered human rights violations or discrimination.

The major reasons for migrating are for family reunion, cultural change, economic and career opportunities, political stability and the appeal of the lifestyle and environment.

ELIGIBILITY UNDER THE SKILLED STREAM

Australia's permanent migration programme encourages people with professional or trade occupations to settle in Australia. More than half of the places on the migration programme are allocated to skilled migrants.

You may apply if you:

- are under 45 years of age at the time of application

- have an occupation that is listed on the Skilled Occupations list (please refer to Appendix 2 for a detailed version of this document)

- have obtained a successful outcome of your skills assessment from the relevant assessing authority in Australia

- have at least 12 to 24 months' recent work experience depending on your occupation

- speak competent English.

IDENTIFYING YOUR OCCUPATION

There are over 400 specific jobs listed on the Skilled Occupations list (SOL) that may qualify a person for permanent migration to Australia. You will need to confirm that you have an occupation that is on this list. The list is grouped into four major categories:

- managers and administrators

- professionals
- associate professionals
- tradespersons and related workers.

It is important to ensure that the occupation that is chosen from the list accurately reflects your experience. Occupations and job titles often differ from country to country, and may be known by different names in Australia.

Many of the job titles on the list cover a wide range of roles and specialisations. If you need to clarify what occupation would be best for you to apply under, you should either contact the relevant assessing authority, or browse through the *Australian Standard Classification of Occupations* book (ASCO).

The Skilled Occupations list also shows:

- the ASCO number for the occupation
- the relevant assessing authority for the occupation
- the number of points allocated for the occupation points test.

HAVING YOUR SKILLS ASSESSED

Before a full migration application can be submitted, the candidate's qualifications, skills, experience and competence in their chosen occupation must be assessed by the relevant assessing authority in Australia. The purpose of this assessment is to ensure that the person is suitably trained, qualified, and experienced to work in the nominated occupation. The government relies on trade associates and professional societies to assess applicants skills. Please refer to the Skilled Occupations list.

The benefit of the skills assessment is that it will help the candidate determine whether it will be worthwhile to submit a full application. Prior to 1999 many people had gone through the effort of preparing a full migration application only to find at the last stages that they did not meet the Australian standards for their occupation, and therefore could not be approved for permanent migration.

Each authority has different procedures to assess a candidate's skills, but in general they will want to see evidence of tertiary or trade qualifications, and proof of any relevant work experience. You should contact the specific authority that deals with your nominated occupation for exact details on how to have your skills assessed. Included below is a general list of information and documentation that the majority of assessing authorities ask for.

Identification
- copy of full-length birth certificate, or
- copy of identification pages of passport
- evidence of change of name (if applicable, e.g., marriage certificate)
- two passport photographs.

Education
- copies of all post-secondary qualifications and certificates (degree, diploma)

- transcripts of courses completed, including details of the duration, date of completion and subjects covered and evidence of the nature and content of the training, describing the content of each subject studied for, the machines, tools and equipment on which you were trained

- registration or licensing membership

- any documentation not in English must be accompanied by an English translation from a certified translator.

Work experience/employment history

In further support for your application, you will need to provide evidence of all your previous and current employment. This should be submitted in the form of a statement of service/reference on company letterhead and signed by a company official. The statement should include the following:

- exact dates when your employment with each specific company commenced and terminated and details of training undertaken and any promotions

- the position/classification in which you were employed

- a full and detailed description of the nature and content of your work tasks and the tools and equipment used.

Where applicable also provide evidence of trade training undertaken during service in the armed forces, e.g. training and employment record (if applicable).

If references for each period of employment are not available (i.e. the company has gone out of business), you should provide:

- certified copies of your annual tax returns
- pay advice/wage slips
- job specifications
- letters of appointment.

Self-employment

If you have been self-employed at any time you should provide the following:

- A personal statement on a properly signed statutory declaration, affidavit or similar legal declaration (with your signature witnessed by a legal authority in your country) providing full details on:
  - the exact commencement and completion date of each period of self-employment
  - the occupations in which you were self-employed
  - the nature and content of the work tasks you personally performed
  - the number of staff employed and their occupations
  - your workshop and the tools and equipment used
  - your business registration certificate.

- At least three statements from suppliers, on letterhead, confirming the nature of business, trading dates, the total amount of all material/equipment purchased over a 12-month period and the types of material equipment supplied.

♦ At least three statements from clients, on letterhead paper, with full details of the work you did for them including dates and the total amount of contracts executed over a 12-month period.

♦ A statement on letterhead from your accountant or legal representative certifying the name and nature of your business, the exact dates of the period of self-employment and the capacity in which you have been self employed.

Payment of fees

All the assessing authorities in Australia charge a fee to carry out a skills assessment. These range from approximately A$100 to A$2,500 depending on the occupation. Most assessing authorities accept credit cards; however, there are still a few who will require their fee to be paid in the form of a bank draft or money order. This will need to be drawn on an Australian bank that will clear in Australia. You will also need to check with the assessing authority who to make the cheque payable to.

How to have your documents correctly certified

This is the stage where many people encounter problems with their applications. Although the following procedures may seem long-winded and pedantic, they are put in place by the assessing authorities to ensure that the information they are receiving is true and factual.

> All documentation submitted to the assessing authority must be certified copies of the originals.

Accordingly, you are required to make photocopies of documents and then take these photocopies, along with the originals, to a person authorised by the Australian Government to certify documents This authorised person will compare the copies with the originals and certify (in the appropriate words) on the copy itself that the photocopy is a true copy of the original document. Failure to adhere to these procedures will render your application invalid, and it will be returned to you, possibly a number of months later, asking you to resubmit it in the correct format.

Persons authorised to certify photocopied documents

◆ solicitor/barrister
◆ justice of the peace/magistrate
◆ notary public
◆ commissioner for oaths/affidavits.

Each certified photocopy must bear the following:

◆ the full name of the authorised person
◆ the person's status, e.g. solicitor, GP
◆ the person's signature
◆ the person's official stamp or seal.

You should not send a photocopy of a document where the certification itself is also part of the photocopy. The certification must always be put onto the photocopied document.

Although the approved person may charge you for this certification service, you should always adhere to the above list of approved persons, as other persons will not be considered acceptable and will result in your application being returned to you without being processed.

How long will it take?

Processing times vary depending on agency procedures and the caseload they have to deal with. Average processing times may range from two to six months, although they will normally issue a letter confirming receipt of the application once they have received it. If the assessing authority requires further information they will normally ask for this by way of a letter. This further information should be promptly forwarded to them to allow them to reach a decision on the case as quickly as possible.

What can I expect the result to be?

If the assessing authority feels that you meet the requirements they will respond with a confirmation letter. They will also give a recommendation on the points that you should be awarded in support of your migration application, though it should be noted that the final decision on occupation points lies with the Department of Immigration and Citizenship (DIAC) processing case officer. For occupations that require Australian registration they may also provide details of any extra registration requirements that will need to be undertaken. This could include conversion courses and/or professional training.

If the assessing authority feels that you do not meet the required standards they will normally provide you with guidance of what will need to be done for their criteria to be met. This might be a period of further work experience or extra studies to gain the necessary qualifications.

Please be aware that some assessing authorities will require practical tests/examinations to be undertaken – some of these can be undertaken in your country of residence, others may require you to travel to Australia.

If the skills assessment is positive the next step will be to clarify what the work experience requirements are for your application.

Clarifying your work experience
If your nominated occupation is worth 60 points you must have been in paid employment in the skilled occupation for at least 12 out of the last 24 months before submitting your full migration application.

If your nominated occupation is worth 40 or 50 points, you must have been in paid employment in a skilled occupation for at least two out of the past three years before applying.

If you are applying under the skills matching or skilled regional sponsored categories you may be eligible with less work experience.

You will be exempt from the work experience require-ments if you have completed an Australian qualification within the six months before submitting your full migration application. This six-month period begins from the date of the completed qualification, and not from the date the qualification was conferred.

Many people applying for a permanent migration visa may not have worked in their nominated occupation for a number of years, and so would not be able to meet the work experience requirements. What some people opt to do is to have their skills assessed, and if the result of this is positive they take employment in their nominated occupation to gain the necessary work experience. After gaining the required experience they can then submit their full migration application.

THE POINTS TEST

There are three categories that require you to pass a points test to be eligible for permanent migration to Australia. They are:

- Skilled Independent
- Skilled Sponsored
- Skilled Regional Sponsored.

Points are awarded for:

- skills
- age
- English language ability
- specific work experience
- occupation in demand (or a job offer)
- Australian qualifications
- spouse skills
- Australian relative (in some circumstances).

Points are also awarded for Australian skilled work experience, or fluency in one of Australia's major community languages.

The pass mark and pool mark

There are two separate score marks on the permanent migration scheme. You must have enough points to meet or exceed the pass mark. The pass mark is taken as the one that is in effect at the time your application is assessed, not from when your application was lodged.

The second mark is the pool mark. If your points score does not reach the pass mark, but meets or exceeds the pool mark, your application will be held by the DIAC for up to two years. If over the two-year period the pass mark is lowered and your points score meets or exceeds the new pass mark, your case will be processed further.

The present pass mark and pool mark scores are listed below:

Visa category	Pass mark	Pool mark
Skilled Independent	120	100
Skilled Sponsored	100	80
Skilled Regional Sponsored	100	None

Skills

The occupation you nominate affects how your skills qualifications are assessed. The occupation must be on the Skilled Occupations list at the time you apply. If the assessing authority deems your skills are suitable for the occupation, you will normally be awarded the allocated points mark from the Skilled Occupations list.

60 points will be awarded to most occupations where training is specific to that occupation. You will normally

need to have a degree or trade certificate qualification as well as experience in your nominated occupation as well as meeting the registration requirements in Australia. For some occupations, work experience will be taken in lieu of formal qualifications.

50 points will be given for more general professional occupations. A qualification equivalent to an Australian degree is normally required, although it does not need to be specific to your nominated occupation.

40 points will be given for other general skilled occupations. These occupations will require the qualification equivalent to an Australian advanced diploma, though they do not need to be specific to the nominated occupation.

Age

Age at time of application	Points
18–29	30
30–34	25
35–39	20
40–44	15

You will need to provide a certified copy of your birth certificate as proof of your age.

ENGLISH LANGUAGE ABILITY

English language ability	IELTS Standard	Points
Vocational English Applicants must have reasonable command of English language, and be able to cope with overall meaning in most situations. They must be able to communicate effectively in their area of employment.	IELTS score of at least 7 on each of the four components in the test – speaking, reading, writing and listening.	25
Competent English Applicants must have an effective command of English language. They must be able to use and understand complex sentences.	IELTS score of at least 6 on each of the four components of test – speaking, reading, writing and listening.	15

All applicants are encouraged to obtain proof of their English language ability.

Points for competent English are automatically awarded to those who were born in and hold passports for the following countries:

- United Kingdom
- United States of America
- Canada
- Republic of Ireland
- New Zealand.

If you were not born and raised in an English-speaking country you may need to provide the following proof:

◆ That you have undertaken post-secondary studies at an institution where the instruction was in English.

◆ Undertake an International English Language Testing System (IELTS) test. You will normally need to take only the general training test, unless you are advised otherwise by your skills-assessing authority. These test results will remain valid for 12 months.

◆ Points for competent English will also be awarded for a pass in the occupational English test or equivalent. This will normally be taken on advice from your assessing authority.

If the DIAC has any doubts about your English language ability they may ask you to take an IELTS test if one has not been done already.

Specific work experience

	Points
If your nominated occupation is worth 60 points and you have worked in that occupation, or a closely related occupation, for at least three out of the four years before you apply.	10
If your nominated occupation is worth 40, 50 or 60 points, and you have worked in skilled employment (any of the occupations on the skilled list), for at least three out of the four years before you apply.	5

To gain points for specific work experience you need to obtain proof by way of employment references and detailed duty statements covering the required period. These may be the same documents that you provide to meet the recent work experience requirements.

Occupation in demand/job offer

There are a number of occupations that are in acute demand in Australia. To encourage people with these skills to apply for permanent migration, the DIAC awards extra points for these occupations. They are also willing to offer further points if the applicant has a job offer in that nominated occupation with an organisation that has employed at least ten people on a full-time basis for the previous two financial years.

	Points
Occupation in demand, but no job offer	15
Occupation in demand with job offer	20

Points will be awarded only if the nominated occupation is on the Migration Occupations in Demand list (MODL) at the time when the application is assessed, not when the application is lodged. As the contents of list can change over time it is advisable to check on DIAC's website *www.immi.gov.au* before submitting the application.

To be eligible to claim extra points for a job offer in this category, evidence will need to be provided to the Department of Immigration and Citizenship proving that an offer has been made. The organisation making the job offer must indicate the number of people that it has employed on a full-time basis for the previous two years. The DIAC rigorously check all applications to ensure that the information is correct.

Australian qualifications

The DIAC recognises that applicants with Australian qualifications have a greater chance of obtaining employment in Australia. Therefore they award extra points for people who have studied for at least 12 months full-time and have completed a qualification in Australia. The qualification must be an Australian post-secondary, degree (or higher) qualification, diploma, advanced diploma or trade qualification. Five points can be claimed in this category. To receive these points a certified copy of the qualification and/or notification of results along with a transcript of the academic record must be submitted with the application.

The Department of Immigration and Citizenship may waive the recent work experience requirements if these Australian qualifications have been completed in the last six months before lodging the migration application. Please note that this six-month period begins from the date of completion of the qualification, and not the date the qualification was conferred.

Spouse skills

If your spouse meets the basic requirements of:

◆ age
◆ English language ability
◆ qualifications

- nominated occupation
- recent work experience
- a suitable skills assessment from a relevant assessing authority,

the DIAC is willing to award an extra 5 points towards the application. Proof that your spouse meets these requirements will be identical to those procedures listed under each of the separate headings.

If your spouse meets these basic requirements you should carefully consider which person to put forward as the main applicant. Normally it will be best for the main applicant to be the person who receives the highest score. If these details are provided, DIAC will be able to assess both people in the relationship, which will help strengthen your application, and give them another option to approve it.

Bonus points
Points may also be claimed for any one of the following.

Australian work experience
If the applicant has worked legally in Australia in one of the occupations on the Skilled Occupations list for at least 12 months in the four years before applying, they may claim 10 extra bonus points. If this work was done when the applicant was on an Australian bridging visa they will not be eligible to claim points.

Fluency in one of Australia's community languages (other than English)
To be eligible to claim the 5 bonus points in this category the applicant must have a professional level of language

skills (written and oral) in one of the community languages listed below. Evidence of their ability must be provided by either:

♦ qualifications from a university where instruction was in one of the listed languages, or

♦ accreditation with National Accreditation Authority for Translators Interpreters (NAATI) at a professional level.

Afrikaans	German	Polish
Albanian	Greek	Portuguese
Arabic (including	Hindi	Romanian
Lebanese)	Hungarian	Russian
Armenian	Indonesian	Serbian
Bengali	Italian	Sinhalese
Bosnian	Japanese	Slovak
Burmese	Khmer	Slovene
Chinese –	Korean	Spanish
Cantonese	Lao	Swedish
Mandarin	Latvian	Tagalog (Filipino)
Croatian	Lithuanian	Tamil
Czech	Macedonian	Thai
Danish	Malaysian	Turkish
Estonian	Maltese	Ukrainian
Fijian	Netherlandic	Urdu
Finnish	(Dutch)	Vietnamese
French	Persian	Yiddish

Health and character checks

Australia has very strict health standards which must be met for any person who is applying to migrate or will be staying in Australia for longer than 12 months. The health standards are designed to ensure that:

+ risks to public health and safety in the Australian community are minimised

+ public expenditure on health and community services is contained

+ Australian residents have access to health and other community services.

All applicants and dependants who intend to migrate must undertake health screening. This screening will include a physical examination, an X-ray, and blood and urine tests.

If the applicant cannot meet the health requirements, the visa applicant will be refused entry unless there are exceptional circumstances not to do so.

Tuberculosis

According to the World Health Organisation, tuberculosis is occurring in epidemic levels globally, and presents a serious infectious public health risk.

All people seeking permanent entry who are over 11 years of age must have a radiological exam for tuberculosis. Any applicants under 11 years of age will also need to undergo the exam if they are suspected of having TB or have a history of contact with a person with TB. If the X-rays show evidence of TB the applicants will be requested to undergo further tests to establish whether or not it is active. If it is active or untreated, the person will need to undergo a course of treatment, and further tests to confirm that the disease has been adequately treated.

Applicants who have evidence of TB, or have had treatment for TB, may be admitted to Australia but will have to provide a health undertaking which will include follow-up monitoring after their arrival in Australia.

Hepatitis B
While the risk of hepatitis B transmission is low, mandatory screening will apply to:

◆ pregnant woman
◆ a child for adoption
◆ an accompanied minor refugee child.

A positive hepatitis B test will not normally lead to a rejection of the application. The person will normally be required to sign a health undertaking.

HIV/AIDS
All migrants over 15 years of age must undergo HIV/AIDS testing. Applicants under 15 years must also be tested if they have been adopted, undergone blood transfusions, or have any other clinical indications.

The health test procedures
The health checks are normally called for by the DIAC processing officer after your full migration application has been submitted. If you pass all the other requirements the DIAC officer will then instruct you to undertake the medicals.

Health checks are normally carried out in the country where the applicant resides, by doctors and radiologists who are approved by the Australian government – these are called panel doctors.

When arranging the medical examinations it is essential that you attend the X-ray examinations before seeing the medical doctor, as the X-rays must be available for them to complete the examination.

Character/police checks

To be granted entry to Australia, applicants must be of good character. To determine this, applicants are asked to provide police clearance checks for each country that they have resided in for more than 12 months in the last ten years whether this has been one lengthy period or a number of short stays which, when added together, equal 12 months or more. It is worth noting that in some countries this process can take from four weeks to over six months.

In certain circumstances applicants may also be required to provide personal details to enable additional character checks to be undertaken. As with the medicals, this information does not need to be provided when you apply.

If you have a substantial criminal record it is likely that your application will be refused. The DIAC's definition of a substantial criminal record is as follows:

- sentenced to either death or life imprisonment
- sentenced to a term of imprisonment for 12 months or more
- sentenced to two or more terms of imprisonment (whether on one or more occasions), where the total of those terms is two years or more
- acquitted of an offence on the grounds of either unsoundness of mind or insanity and, as a result, the person has been detained in a facility or institution.

Visa limits

At any stage the Australian government may apply limits (caps) to the number of visas granted each year, or suspend processing applications. If a cap is applied the application will be processed but the visa will not be granted in the year that the visa limits are reached.

Family members

If your other family members are also applying for a visa you will need to decide who to put forward as the primarily applicant. This will generally be the person who has the best chance of meeting the migration requirements. Other family members such as spouses, dependent children or dependent relatives should be included in the same application so you pay only one charge. Children who are born after an application is made, but before a decision has been reached, will automatically be included in the parents' application. If this circumstance arises the Australian mission must be notified of the details of the newborn child. In some circumstances a spouse or dependent child can be added to an application, although they will also need to meet certain visa requirements.

Can I lodge more than one application?

If more than one visa is applied for, and approved, the last visa issued will normally be the one that is valid. Thus, any previous visa granted will be null and void. For further advice and clarification the relevant Australian mission should be contacted.

Withdrawing an application

If you wish to withdraw an application, notice must be lodged in writing with the Australian mission. Any charges that you have paid to have your case processed will not usually be refunded.

CONTACTING THE AUSTRALIAN MISSION

Change of address
It is the applicant's responsibility to inform the Australian mission of any change of address that occurs for periods longer than 14 days. The Australian mission must be informed of the new address and how long you will be staying there. Correspondence will always be sent to the last known address provided and deemed to have been received within 21 days of writing.

Correspondence regarding the application can also be sent to another person or agent (details of this representative must be supplied on a Form 956), and it will be taken that the applicant has received any letters sent to that person. The Australian mission must also be informed if you intend to travel to Australia while the application is being processed

Change of circumstances
The Australian mission must be informed of any changes of circumstances; for example, a serious illness, change in marital status, the birth of a child, or if a new passport is obtained, as soon as possible and practical. The visa may be cancelled if incorrect information is supplied or you fail to advise the DIAC that some of the information is no longer correct. This information should be supplied to the Australian mission on the Form 1022.

Supplying extra information

Additional information can be provided in writing at any stage before a decision has been made on the application. In some circumstances DIAC will request or invite you to provide additional information. You will be given a date by which to respond. After that date the application will continue to be considered whether or not you have provided the information requested. DIAC will not delay the decision-making process if the applicant says they may, or will, give more information later.

Interviews

The Australian mission may invite you to attend an interview. You will need to agree on the time and date with a DIAC representative. If you do not attend the interview the application will be processed, and a decision will be made on the basis of the information available. You may be given another opportunity to arrange an interview; however, the Australian mission is not obliged to do so.

How your application is processed

All applications are decided two factors: firstly the information that is provided by you, and secondly the law at the time it was submitted. Applicants should be aware that the government may change the pass mark and pool mark at any time, and this may affect the application.

It is imperative that you thoroughly check through the application and documentation before submitting them for consideration. While it can be a time-consuming and frustrating process gathering together all the information, it must be submitted in the required formats, otherwise it will lead to delays in the processing of the case.

5

Family Categories

FIANCÉ CATEGORY

Are you engaged to be married to an Australian citizen, Australian permanent resident or eligible New Zealand citizen? If applying under the Fiancé category you will need to demonstrate that your relationship is genuine. You will have to show that you intend to marry your fiancé within nine months from the date you are granted a visa and give an undertaking that you intend to live with your partner as their spouse. A further requirement that you and your fiancé are known to each other is included in the criteria. To satisfy the requirements of this category both you and your fiancé must be aged over 18 years.

For the Fiancé category, your application must be lodged outside of Australia and the applicant at the time of applying must also be outside of Australia.

There are three stages to this application process for the Fiancé category.

Stage One – Prospective marriage temporary visa

The first stage allows you to apply for a temporary visa. You will need to provide evidence in support of your relationship and complete a medical examination, and provide character checks/police clearances from any country you have lived in for more than 12 months in the last ten years. If the DIAC wants to further assess the information you have supplied in support of your application they may request you and your fiancé to attend an interview.

If this first stage is approved you will be granted a temporary visa valid for nine months from the date it is issued. Within that time you must travel to Australia, get married and then apply for the Spouse Temporary category.

Stage Two – Spouse temporary visa

You must be in Australia when you apply for stage two. You apply for this after your marriage. You must be in Australia when you apply, complete the application forms, pay the application fee, and provide documentary evidence in support of your marriage demonstrating that it is genuine and continuing.

If successful, you will be granted a temporary visa until a decision on your application for a permanent visa is decided. This temporary visa allows for multiple re-entry to Australia.

Stage Three – Spouse permanent visa

Stage three will commence approximately two years after you lodge your application for Spouse category after your initial Fiancé category application.

At this time DIAC will require documentary evidence from you and your spouse that your relationship is genuine and continuing. This will consist of statements from friends or family who know you, and evidence that your relationship is continuing and genuine, and an Australian Police clearance if you have been living in Australia for more than 12 months. You may be invited to attend an interview by DIAC. If you meet the requirements your permanent resident's visa will be granted. You must be in Australia at the time the visa is granted.

Prospective spouse document checklist

The following documentation should be forwarded to the Australian High Commission in your country of legal residence together with the completed Forms 47SP and 40SP.

To be eligible for this category of visa you must be able to show evidence that you genuinely intend to marry your fiancé(e) within nine months from the date you are granted a visa, and intend to then live with your partner as their spouse. You should provide evidence of the following:

- that you have a celebrant in place to marry you
- you and your fiancé(e) have met and are personally known to each other.

Joint relationship history

1. A joint signed statement outlining the nature and duration of your relationship:

- how, when and where you met
- details of when you became engaged to marry
- how you support each other emotionally and financially (if applicable)
- dates when you met each other's families
- dates of joint holidays and travel
- reasons for any periods of separation
- your future plans.

You should also supply any documentary evidence available of the length of time you have been a couple, photographs, cards and letters/emails and if you have lived together at any time, utility bills/bank statements/ council tax details, etc.

2. Four Statutory Declarations from next of kin/ close relatives or friends stating the following:

- their relationship to you both
- how long they have known you as a couple
- whether they regard you as a genuine couple
- any other information regarding your relationship that they feel is appropriate.

NB: Statutory Declarations must be signed, stamped and witnessed by a solicitor.

Main applicant

- certified copy of full-length birth certificate for each

person included in the application.

- certified copy of marriage certificate (if applicable)
- certified copies of divorce papers (if applicable)
- certified copies of adoption papers (if applicable).

NB: If there are children from a previous marriage or relationship included in the application, a Statutory Declaration giving permission for the child to leave the UK must be provided by the child's/children's other parent.

Identification

- certified copy of the identification pages of passport
- four passport photos for main applicant and any children included in the application (name to be written on reverse of photos).

If you have been self-employed you should provide a letter from your accountant confirming the periods of self-employment together with evidence of tax and NI contributions.

Sponsorship (Form 40SP)

Your Australian partner must complete Form 40SP and supply the following documentation:

- certified copy of birth certificate
- certified copy of marriage certificate (if applicable)
- certified copy of Australian citizenship
- certified copy of proof of address in Australia (utility bills) (if applicable)
- certified copy of proof of employment (letter from employer/wage slips)

♦ statement confirming that your partner fully supports your application both emotionally and financially.

Police clearances

Each person included in the application who is over the age of 16 years will be required to obtain a Police Clearance certificate from the Metropolitan Police Authority. Police Clearances must also be obtained for any country that you have lived in for more than 12 months in the last ten years.

Medical and radiological examinations

The main applicant will be required to undergo medical and radiological examinations by an appointed medical practitioner.

The Australian High Commission is accepting what they call 'front end loaded' applications. Basically, this means that you provide police clearances and medical examination results at the time of submission of your application.

This does not give any guarantee that your application will be successful, but it does mean that a decision is likely to be made within around three weeks of application as opposed to three to six months should you wait until these are requested.

PARTNER CATEGORY

The Partner category covers relationships where you are living with an Australian citizen, permanent resident or eligible New Zealand citizen. For this category you must satisfy the genuine relationship requirement. This means that you and your partner must have a mutual commitment to a shared life together without marriage. This commitment must be to the exclusion of any other spouse or partner relationships. You will need to demonstrate that you and your partner are living together, and that you do not live separately or apart on a permanent basis. The relationship with you and your partner must have existed for a minimum period of 12 months before the date of application.

At the time of application you and your partner must be at least 18 years of age.

This category of application is processed in two stages.

Stage One – Partner temporary visa

The first stage will assess your eligibility for a temporary visa under the Partner category. You will need to supply documentary evidence in support of your relationship, undergo a medical examination and submit character clearances/police clearances for any country in which you have lived for more than 12 months in the last ten years.

If your application is approved at this first stage you will be granted a temporary visa until the time that your application for a permanent visa is decided.

Stage Two – Partner permanent visa

Stage two will begin approximately two years after the time that you submitted your temporary visa application. At this time DIAC will assess your eligibility for a permanent visa.

You will be required to supply documentary evidence in support of your relationship. Your relationship must be genuine and continuing. You will require declarations from friends and family supporting the circumstances of your relationship.

If you have been living in Australia for more than 12 months you will need to supply an Australian Police clearance. You and your partner may also be requested to attend an interview by the DIAC.

Partner category checklist

The following documentation should be forwarded to the Australian High Commission together with the completed Forms 47SP and 40SP. Australia's migration regulations stipulate that a partner relationship is one where the parties have cohabited for at least one year prior to the lodgement of their application.

Joint financial information

- certified copies of joint bank account
- wills or life assurance policies made out with the other partner nominated as the principal beneficiary
- certified copies of joint property ownership
- certified copies of joint savings plans or investments.

NB: If the partner has no independent income, evidence must be provided that they are supported by the other partner and have access to their partner's finances.

Joint relationship history

1. A joint signed statement outlining the nature and duration of your relationship:

- how, when and where you met
- dates and reasons you commenced cohabitation
- your domestic arrangements
- how you support each other emotionally and financially
- dates when you met each other's families
- dates of joint holidays and travel
- reasons for any periods of separation
- your reasons for not marrying
- your future plans.

Four Statutory Declarations from next of kin/close relatives or friends stating the following:

- their relationship to you both
- how long they have known you as a couple
- whether they regard you as partners
- any other information regarding your relationship that they feel is appropriate.

NB: Statutory Declarations must be signed, stamped and witnessed by a solicitor.

3. Certified copies of the following evidence must also be provided:

- joint mortgage agreement/tenancy agreement
- joint utility bills – telephone, gas, electricity, cable TV, etc.
- proof of purchase – household items
- proof of joint travel
- NHS cards
- official letters depicting joint address

- bank statements
- drivers' licences
- council tax documentation.

The aforementioned list is a 'wish list'. It is unlikely that you will have all of the above; however, you must supply as much evidence of your partnership as possible.

Main applicant
- certified copy of full-length birth certificate for each person included in the application
- certified copies of divorce papers (if applicable)
- certified copies of adoption papers (if applicable).

NB: If there are children from a previous marriage or relationship included in the application, a Statutory Declaration giving permission for the child to leave the UK must be provided by the child's/children's other parent.

Identification
- certified copy of the identification pages of passport
- four passport photos for main applicant and any children included in the application and two passport photos of the sponsor (name to be written on reverse of photos).

Education
- certified copies of all tertiary qualifications and certificates for the main applicant.

Work experience/employment history
Periods of employment in the last five years must be supported by:

- certified copies of reference, on company letterhead, stating occupation, dates of employment
- list of duties and responsibilities.

If references for each period of employment are not available, you should provide certified copies of:

- P60s
- pay advice/wage slips
- job specifications
- letters of appointment.

If you have been self-employed you should provide a letter from your accountant confirming the periods of self-employment together with evidence of tax and NI contributions

Your Australian partner must supply the following information:

- certified copy of birth certificate
- certified copy of marriage certificate
- certified copy of Australian citizenship
- certified copy of proof of address in Australia (utility bills) (if applicable)
- certified copy of proof of employment (letter from employer/wage slips)
- statement confirming that your partner fully supports your application both emotionally and financially.

Police clearances

Each person included in the application who is over the age of 16 years will be required to obtain a Police

Clearance certificate from the Police Authority. Police Clearances must also be obtained for any country that you have lived in for more than 12 months in the last ten years.

Medical and radiological examinations

The main applicant will be required to undergo a medical and radiological examination by an appointed medical practitioner.

SPOUSE CATEGORY

The Spouse category covers relationships where you are married to an Australian citizen, permanent resident or eligible New Zealand citizen. For this category you must satisfy the genuine relationship requirement. This means that you and your partner must have a mutual commitment to a shared life. You will need to demonstrate that you and your partner are in a genuine relationship and that you have not married solely for the purposes of migration. The relationship between you and your partner must have been for a minimum period of 12 months before the date of application. At the time of application you and your partner must be at least 18 years of age. This category of application is processed in two stages.

Stage one – Spouse temporary visa

The first stage will assess your eligibility for a temporary visa under the Spouse category. You will need to supply documentary evidence in support of your relationship, undergo a medical examination and submit character clearances/police clearances for any country in which you have lived for more than 12 months in the last ten years.

If your application is approved at this first stage you will be granted a temporary visa until the time that your application for a permanent visa is decided. However, if you have been married for more than five years you may be provided with a permanent visa in the first instance.

Stage two – Spouse permanent visa

Stage two will begin approximately two years after the time that you submitted your temporary visa application. At this time the DIAC will assess your eligibility for a permanent visa.

You will be required to supply documentary evidence in support of your relationship. Your relationship must be genuine and continuing.

You will require declarations from friends and family supporting the circumstances of your relationship. If you have been living in Australia for more than 12 months you will need to supply an Australian police clearance. You and your partner may also be requested to attend an interview by the DIAC.

Spouse category document checklist

The following documentation should be forwarded to the Australian High Commission together with the completed Forms 47SP and 40SP.

Joint financial information

- certified copies of joint bank account
- wills or life assurance policies made out with the other partner nominated as the principal beneficiary

- certified copies of joint property ownership
- certified copies of joint savings plans or investments.

NB: If the partner has no independent income, evidence must be provided that they are supported by the other partner and have access to their partner's finances.

Joint relationship history

1. A joint signed statement outlining the nature and duration of your relationship:

- how, when and where you met
- when and why you decided to marry
- your domestic arrangements
- how you support each other emotionally and financially
- reasons for any periods of separation
- your future plans.

2. Two Statutory Declarations from next of kin/close relatives or friends who are Australian stating the following:

- their relationship to you both
- how long they have known you as a couple
- that your marriage is genuine
- any other information regarding your relationship that they feel is appropriate.

NB: Statutory Declarations must be signed, stamped and witnessed by a solicitor.

Main applicant

- ◆ certified copy of full-length birth certificate for each person included in the application
- ◆ certified copy of marriage certificate
- ◆ certified copies of divorce papers (if applicable)
- ◆ certified copies of adoption papers (if applicable).

NB: If there are children from a previous marriage or relationship included in the application, a Statutory Declaration giving permission for the child to leave the UK must be provided by the child's/children's other parents.

Identification

- ◆ certified copy of the identification pages of passport
- ◆ four passport photos for main applicant and any children included in the application; two passport photos are required from the sponsor (name to be written on reverse of photos).

Education

Certified copies of all tertiary qualifications and certificates for the main applicant.

Work experience/employment history

Periods of employment in the last five years must be supported by:

- ◆ certified copies of reference, on company letterhead, stating occupation, dates of employment and a list of duties and responsibilities.

If references for each period of employment are not available you should provide certified copies of:

- P60s
- pay advice/wage slips
- job specifications
- letters of appointment.

If you have been self-employed you should provide a letter from your accountant confirming the periods of self-employment together with evidence of tax and NI contributions.

Your Australian partner must supply the following documentation:

- certified copy of birth certificate
- certified copy of marriage certificate
- certified copy of Australian citizenship
- certified copy of proof of address in Australia (utility bills) (if applicable)
- certified copy of proof of employment (letter from employer/wage slips)
- statement confirming that your partner fully supports your application both emotionally and financially.

Police clearances
Each person included in the application who is over the age of 16 years will be required to obtain a Police Clearance certificate from the Police Authority. Police clearances must also be obtained for any country that you have lived in for more than 12 months in the last ten years.

Medical and radiological examinations
The main applicant will be required to undergo a medical

and radiological examination by an appointed medical practitioner. The Australian High Commission is accepting what they call 'front end loaded' applications. Basically, this means that you provide police clearances and medical examination results at the time of submission of your application.

This does not give any guarantee that your application will be successful, although it does mean that a decision is likely to be made within six weeks of application, as opposed to four to six months should you wait until these are requested.

INTERDEPENDENT PARTNER CATEGORY

The Interdependent Partner category covers same-sex relationships where you are living with an Australian citizen. For this category you must satisfy the genuine relationship requirement. This means that you and your partner must have a mutual commitment to a shared life together. This commitment must be to the exclusion of any spouse or any other interdependent relationships. You will need to demonstrate that you and your partner are living together and that you do not live separately or apart on a permanent basis. The relationship between you and your partner must have been for a minimum period of 12 months before the date of application.

Under this category if you have compassionate circumstances due to difficulties living together or co-habitating in the country you have been living in prior to applying then this can be brought to the attention of the DIAC office.

At the time of application you and your partner must be at least 18 years of age.

This category of application is processed in two stages.

Stage one – Interdependency temporary visa

The first stage will assess your eligibility for a temporary visa under the Interdependent category. You will need to supply documentary evidence in support of your relationship, undergo a medical examination and submit character clearances/police clearances for any country in which you have lived for more than 12 months in the last ten years.

If your application is approved at this first stage you will be granted a temporary visa until the time that your application for a permanent visa is decided.

Stage two – Interdependency permanent visa

Stage two will begin approximately two years after the time that you submitted your temporary visa application. At this time DIAC will assess your eligibility for a permanent visa.

You will be required to supply documentary evidence in support of your relationship. Your relationship must be genuine and continuing. You will require declarations from friends and family supporting the circumstances of your relationship. If you have been living in Australia for more than 12 months you will need to supply an Australian police clearance. You and your partner may also be requested to attend an interview by DIAC. If you and your partner have been in your relationship for five years or more you may not need to fulfil the normal two-year temporary visa period.

Interdependent category checklist

Australia's migration regulations stipulate that an inter-dependent relationship is one where the parties have cohabited for at least one year prior to the lodgement of their application.

The following documentation should be forwarded to the Australian High Commission together with the completed Forms 47SP and 40SP.

Joint financial information

- certified copies of joint bank account
- wills or life assurance policies made out with the other partner nominated as the principle beneficiary
- certified copies of joint property ownership
- certified copies of joint savings plans or investments.

NB: If the partner has no independent income, evidence must be provided that they are supported by the other partner and have access to their partner's finances.

Joint relationship history

1. A joint signed statement outlining the nature and duration of your relationship:

- how, when and where you met
- dates and reasons you commenced cohabitation
- your domestic arrangements
- how you support each other emotionally and financially

- dates when you met each other's families
- dates of joint holidays and travel
- reasons for any periods of separation
- your future plans.

2. Four Statutory Declarations from next of kin/close relatives or friends stating the following:

- their relationship to you both
- how long they have known you as a couple
- that they regard you as a genuine couple
- any other information regarding your relationship that they feel is appropriate.

NB: Statutory Declarations must be signed, stamped and witnessed by a solicitor.

3. Certified copies of the following evidence must also be provided:

- joint mortgage agreement/tenancy agreement
- joint utility bills – telephone, gas, electricity, cable TV, etc.
- proof of purchase – household items
- proof of joint travel
- NHS cards
- official letters depicting joint address
- bank statements
- council tax documentation.

The aforementioned is a 'wish list'. You may not be able to supply all of the above; however, you should supply as much as you can.

Main applicant

- certified copy of full-length birth certificate for each person included in the application
- certified copies of adoption papers (if applicable).

NB: If there are children from a previous marriage or relationship included in the application, a Statutory Declaration giving permission for the child to leave the UK must be provided by the child's/children's other parent.

Identification

- certified copy of the identification pages of passport
- four passport photos for main applicant and any children included in the application; two passport photos of the sponsor (name to be written on reverse of photos).

Education

- Certified copies of all tertiary qualifications and certificates for the main applicant.

Work experience/employment history

Periods of employment in the last five years must be supported by:

- certified copies of reference, on company letterhead, stating occupation, dates of employment and a list of duties and responsibilities.

If references for each period of employment are not available, you should provide certified copies of:

- P60s
- pay advice/wage slips
- job specifications
- letters of appointment.

If you have been self-employed you should provide a letter from your accountant confirming the periods of self-employment together with evidence of tax and NI contributions.

Your Australian partner must supply the following information:

- certified copy of birth certificate
- certified copy of Australian citizenship
- certified copy of proof of address in Australia (utility bills) (if applicable)
- certified copy of proof of employment (letter from employer/wage slips)
- statement confirming that your partner fully supports your application both emotionally and financially.

Police clearances

Each person included in the application who is over the age of 16 years will be required to obtain a Police Clearance certificate from the Police Authority. Police clearances must also be obtained for any country that you have lived in for more than 12 months in the last ten years.

Medical and radiological examinations

The main applicant will be required to undergo a medical and radiological examination by an appointed medical practitioner. You will be advised by the Australian mission processing your application when these are required.

PARENT MIGRATION

There are four different categories of visa available for parents residing outside of Australia who wish to reside in Australia. There are two classes of visa, the Parent visa and the Contributory Parent visa. The main difference between these two classes of visa is that those applying under the Contributory Parent visa class are required to make a higher contribution toward their future health costs.

The two offshore Contributory Parent visa subclasses are as follows:

◆ Subclass 143 Contributory Parent (Migrant) visa
◆ Subclass 173 Contributory Parent (Temporary) visa.

The threshold requirements for the Contributory Parent visa categories are substantially similar to the Parent visa categories.

Both categories will have the same first Visa Application Charge (VAC) which is payable at the time of application; this should be confirmed at the time of application. The key differences would be the level of the second VAC (payable before a visa is granted) and the level and duration of the Assurance of Support bond.

There are significantly more places available under the Contributory Parent visa categories than for the Parent visa categories. This recognises the fact that Contributory Parent visa applicants are willing to pay a significantly higher second VAC as a contribution to their ongoing health costs.

There are two payment options for Contributory Parent visa applicants:

◆ Permanent visa: pay a A$31,555 second VAC per person (at 1 October 2007, A$1,365 for dependants under 18).

◆ Temporary visa: pay a A$18,935 second VAC per person (at 1 October 2007, A$1,365 for dependants under 18), which would entitle parents to a two-year temporary residence visa including Medicare access and work rights. During that period, parents may apply at any time for a permanent visa, at which time the remaining payment is required (nil for dependants under 18).

The Contributory Parent visa category also requires a ten-year, A$10,000 Assurance of Support bond for main applicants and A$4,000 for adult secondary applicants (for temporary visa holders, this is payable during processing of the permanent visa).

There are two further categories of visa available: the Parent visa and the Aged Parent visa. Applications made within this visa class will take substantially longer to process than those of the contributory classes.

The basic criteria for these visa categories are based on the same principles as the contributory scheme; the main difference is that you are not required to pay the second VAC.

Aged parent

You can apply as an aged parent if you are old enough to be granted an Australian Age pension. You must be the aged parent of a child who is an Australian citizen, Australian permanent resident or eligible New Zealand citizen.

Your child must be resident in Australia for at least two years before your application is submitted. Your child will have to sponsor or nominate you. Under this category you will also require an assurance of support.

You must pass the balance of family test (see below).

Working aged parent

A working aged parent is an applicant who at the time of applying is not at an age where they would be granted an Australian age pension. You must be the working aged parent of a child who is an Australian citizen, Australian permanent resident or eligible New Zealand citizen. Your child must have been resident in Australia for at least two years at the time of application.

To be eligible for this category you must pass the balance of family test. You will need to be sponsored by an appropriate person and you will need to provide an assurance of support.

Age requirements

An aged parent is one who is old enough to be granted an

Australian Age pension. If you are married only one parent needs to be aged.

Qualifying ages for Australian Age pension	
For men – the qualifying age is 65 years	
For women – the qualifying age for women depends on their date of birth	
Date of birth	Qualifying age
Before 31 December 1942 (from 30 June 2005)	62.5
1 January 1943–30 June 1944 (from 1 January 2006–30 June 2007)	63
1 July 1944–31 December 1945 (from 1 January 2008–30 June 2009)	63.5
1 January 1946–30 June 1947 (from 1 January 2010–30 June 2011)	64
1 July 1947–31 December 1948 (from 1 January 2012–30 June 2013)	64.5
1 January 1949 and later (from 1 January 2014 an onwards)	65

BALANCE OF FAMILY TEST

For parent applications you must pass the Balance of Family test:

◆ at least half of your children must live in Australia, or
◆ you must have more children living in Australia than in any one other country.

The test is to measure your family links to Australia compared with your family links elsewhere.

Sponsorship/nomination

If you are making your application outside of Australia, you and any dependants included in the application must be sponsored. The sponsor will be required to give a written undertaking to provide support for you during your first two years in Australia, including accommodation and financial assistance if required to meet your family's reasonable living needs.

If you are making your application in Australia, you and any dependants included in the application must be nominated. The nominator does not have to give the same undertaking as a sponsor; however, they are still expected to provide assistance to you and your family during the first two years that you are resident in Australia.

A sponsor/nominator must be aged 18 years or over.

If you are making your application outside Australia, generally you must be sponsored by your child (natural, adopted or step-child) who is a settled Australian citizen, Australian permanent resident or a settled eligible New Zealand citizen. The definition of settled for this purpose is being resident in Australia for the past two years at the time of application.

Assurance of support

All applicants making an application for a Parent visa, whether Aged Parent or Working Aged Parent, will require an assurance of support.

Your sponsor and assurer do not need to be the same

person. The person giving an assurance of support, however, must be over 18 and an adult Australian citizen, Australian permanent resident or eligible New Zealand citizen who is usually resident in Australia and financially able to support the sponsored person and demonstrate their ability to repay certain social security payments should they have been made to people covered by the assurance.

The assurance of support is a commitment to provide financial support to the person applying to migrate so that the applicant will not have to rely on any form of government support. It is also a legal commitment by the person to repay the Commonwealth of Australia any social security payments that may have been made to the person covered by the assurance. The assurance lasts for a stipulated period from the date of arrival in Australia.

An assurer must be able to demonstrate that their taxable income is sustained at a level that would allow them to provide financial support to the applicants whom they assure and also that they would be able to repay any debt incurred by payment of social security payments during the stipulated period. The assurer will have to undergo an income test. You should confirm the required level of income with Centrelink at the time of application.

Parent categories document checklist
The following documentation should be supplied together with the completed Forms 47PA/47PT and 40.

Relationship

- certified copies of full-length birth certificates for each person included in the application
- certified copy of marriage certificate
- certified copies of divorce papers (if applicable)
- certified copies of adoption papers (if applicable).

Identification

- certified copies of the identification pages of passports
- four passport photos for each person included in the application (name to be written on reverse of photos).

Sponsorship (Form 40)

Evidence of your relationship to your child/children in Australia, and they will be required to complete the Form 40 with the following:

- certified copy of birth certificate (proving relationship to you)
- certified copy of marriage certificate
- certified copy of Australian citizenship
- proof of address (utility bills)
- proof of employment (letter from employer/wage slips).

Assurance of support

Your sponsor must undertake to assist you with accommodation and financial support if necessary, for a stipulated period immediately following your entry into Australia. It will also be necessary for your sponsor to lodge an assurance of support with an approved banking institution in Australia. You will be advised when this is required.

Balance of Family test

If all your children are living in Australia, your application will receive priority over applications where only an equal number are in Australia and an equal number living overseas. To support the Balance of Family test you must provide the following evidence from all your children:

◆ full birth certificates proving their relationship to you
◆ adoption certificates (if applicable)
◆ citizenship documents or residency stamps in passports for their usual country of residence
◆ proof of registration on the electoral roll
◆ pay and employment advice.

Police clearances

Each person included in the application who is over the age of 16 years will be required to obtain a Police Clearance certificate from the Police Authority. Police clearances must also be obtained for any country that you have lived in for more than 12 months in the last ten years.

Medical and radiological examinations

Everyone included in the application will be required to undergo a medical and radiological examination by an appointed medical practitioner. You will be advised by the Australian mission processing your application when these are required

⑥

Employer-Sponsored Migration

There are four categories for employer-sponsored migration to Australia:

- the Employer Nomination scheme
- the Regional Sponsored Migration scheme
- Labour agreements
- the Invest Australia Supported Skills program.

THE EMPLOYER NOMINATION SCHEME (ENS)

This has been developed to allow Australian employers to recruit permanent, highly skilled staff from overseas or people temporarily in Australia, when the employers have been unable to fill a vacancy from within the Australian labour market or through their own training programmes.

The ENS process has two stages:

- nomination by an employer
- the nominee's application for a visa.

Requirements for an employer

◆ They have a need for a paid employee, the business is located in Australia and it is operated by the employer.

◆ The vacancy requires the appointment of a highly skilled person.

◆ If applicable, the highly skilled person is eligible for any mandatory licensing, registration or professional body membership where required.

◆ The position is a full-time, fixed-term appointment of at least three years, which does not exclude the possibility of renewal.

◆ The employer has a satisfactory training record or, for a new business, must make satisfactory provision for future training.

◆ The employer must have demonstrated that the position cannot be filled through the Australian labour market, unless the position is on the Migrant Occupations in Demand list (MODL).

◆ The terms and conditions of employment must be in accordance with the standards for working conditions provided under Australian industrial laws.

Requirements for visa nominee

In general terms, the visa application will be assessed against the following:

◆ the nominee has the skills relevant to the nominated position

- the nominee meets the definition of a highly skilled person
- the nominee is able to satisfy any mandatory licensing, registration or professional membership requirements

- the employment as outlined in the approved nomination is still available

- the nominee is less than 45 years of age

- the nominee has vocational English language ability

- the nominee and all family unit members meet mandatory health and character requirements.

THE REGIONAL SPONSORED MIGRATION SCHEME (RSMS)

The RSMS is designed to help employers in regional or low population growth areas of Australia who have been unable to fill skilled vacancies from the indigenous labour market.

An employer can take part in the scheme if their business is in any area except Brisbane, Gold Coast, Newcastle, Sydney, Wollongong, Melbourne and Perth.

Employers considering nominating persons under the RSMS may identify suitable nominees in various ways, including:

- through their efforts in testing the local labour market
- personal contact and/or experience with the nominee
- recommendation from third parties
- through the department's Skill Matching programme.

Skill Matching Database

Skill matching is made possible by the Skill Matching Database. It contains the educational, occupational and personal details of Skilled-Independent category applicants and Skill Matching visa applicants.

The Skill Matching Database is updated monthly and distributed to all State and Territory governments and to a network of regional development authorities.

Employers can use the database to identify suitable applicants for nomination under the RSMS or labour agreements. Applicants nominated from the database do not need to lodge a further visa application.

The RSMS process consists of three stages:

1. certification of the nomination/vacancy
2. nomination by the employer
3. nominee's application for a visa.

Requirements for certification

In general terms, the employer must be able to demonstrate to a certifying body that:

- the position is a genuine full-time vacancy
- it is available for at least two consecutive years
- it requires qualifications equivalent to at least Australian diploma level (this includes trade certificates)
- the position cannot be filled from the local labour market
- employment and remuneration are in accordance with Australian industrial laws

- there is, or will be, an employment contract or letter of appointment covering the position.

Employer nomination assessment

The completed and certified nomination needs to be forwarded to the relevant department business centre, which needs to be satisfied that:

- the nomination has been certified by a regional certifying body
- all the above conditions were met.

Visa nominee requirements

In general terms, the visa application will be assessed against the following:

- that the nominee has the relevant qualifications equivalent to at least an Australian diploma
- that the nominee is able to satisfy any mandatory licensing, registration or professional membership requirements
- that the position is for a fixed term of at least two years (supported by evidence of a contract)
- that the nominee is less than 45 years of age
- that the nominee has functional English language ability
- that the nominee and all family unit members meet mandatory health and character requirements.

Visa cancellation provisions

Since 1 July 2001, visa cancellation provisions apply where:

♦ the employee has not commenced employment with the employer within six months of arriving in Australia (or after visa grant if already in Australia), or

♦ where an employee has left the employer within the two-year period for reasons within their control.

Cancellation of a visa will not occur where a nominating employer terminates an employee's contract within the two-year period, provided the employee has made a genuine effort to complete the two years with the approved employer.

If the employee's visa is cancelled, the visas for people who accompanied the employee to Australia, such as family members, will also be cancelled.

LABOUR AGREEMENTS (LA)

Labour agreements allow Australian employers to recruit (either permanently or temporarily) a specified number of workers from overseas in response to identified or emerging labour market (or skill) shortages in the indigenous labour market. They provide an avenue for either permanent or temporary entry to Australia. They are also designed to ensure that overseas recruitment supports the longer-term improvement of employment and training opportunities for Australians.

Employers or industrial associations are required to make commitments to the employment, education, training and career opportunities of Australians as part of the agreement.

After the agreement has been negotiated, the process consists of two stages:

1. nomination by the employer
2. nominee's application for a visa.

Nomination by the employer

Temporary entry
The employer submits the relevant application form to the business centre managing that labour agreement.

Permanent entry
The employer submits the relevant application form to the business centre managing that labour agreement.

The nomination will be assessed to determine whether:

◆ the nomination is in accordance with the relevant labour agreement

◆ the vacancy falls within the agreed ceiling for the agreement

◆ the terms and conditions of employment are in accordance with the agreement

◆ the nominee is under 45 years of age

◆ the nominee has the qualifications and skills (including

English language skills) specified in the labour agreement.

Nominee's application for a visa

In general terms, the visa application will be assessed against the following:

◆ that the nominee has the qualifications, skills (including English language skills) and experience specified in the agreement

◆ that the nominee is able to satisfy any mandatory licensing, registration or professional membership requirements under the labour agreement

◆ that the nominee is less than 45 years of age

◆ that the nominee and all family unit members meet mandatory health and character requirements.

Skill Matching Database

Employers wishing to nominate visa applicants under a labour agreement can utilise the Skill Matching Database to identify suitably qualified workers. The Skill Matching Database contains the educational, occupational and personal details of Skilled–Independent category applicants and Skill Matching visa applicants.

Applicants nominated from the database under a labour agreement do not need to lodge a further visa application.

The database is updated monthly and distributed to all State and Territory governments and to a network of regional development authorities.

INVEST AUSTRALIA SUPPORT SKILLS (IASS)

The IASS programme is designed to encourage international firms to choose Australia as a location for foreign direct investment. It allows companies that make a significant investment in Australia to bring out essential key expatriate managerial and specialist employees from within the company group (this programme replaced Regional Headquarters agreements from 1 July 2002).

Agreements are for three years, although individual visas, once granted, may extend beyond the period of the agreement. IASS agreements are for permanent and/or temporary entry of key managerial and specialist employees.

Companies wishing to obtain visas for very small numbers of personnel, or which are seeking staff for existing investments, should access other business immigration programmes.

Applicants must meet at least one of the following four criteria for investments of strategic significance to be eligible for the IASS programme:

◆ the project will boost Australian industry innovation through increasing research, development and commercialisation capability, the new application of skills and knowledge technology transfer, and Cluster development

◆ the project will have significant economic benefit to regional Australia taking account a region's investment needs

◆ the project's estimated investments is in excess of A$50 million and thus inherently makes a significant contribution to economic growth, employment and/or infrastructure

◆ the company is establishing a regional headquarters or regional operating centre in Australia.

The purpose for the establishment of IASS agreements is different from standard labour agreements in that:

◆ visas granted under IASS agreements are to enable the transfer to Australia of key managerial and specialist employees of the company group

◆ visa applications to which an IASS agreement applies receive priority over applications made under standard labour agreements.

IASS agreements provide for either permanent or temporary entry to Australia. The company submits its proposal to Invest Australia in the Department of Industry, Tourism and Resources (DITR).

Invest Australia will liaise with DIAC (and other government departments, if necessary) if it decides to proceed with the company's application.

An IASS agreement becomes effective once it has been signed by all parties to the agreement – the manager of Invest Australia, a company representative, and finally, a delegate of the Minister for Immigration and Citizenship.

After an agreement has been negotiated, the process consists of two stages: nomination by the employer; and the nominee's application for a visa.

Provisional Visas

SKILLED – REGIONAL SPONSORED (SUBCLASS 475)

The Skilled–Regional Sponsored visa was implemented on 1 September 2007 and has extensively replaced the Skilled Independent Regional and Skilled Designated Area Sponsored visas. The main aim of the Skilled–Regional Sponsored visa is to assist in the development of regional Australia through skilled migration. The Skilled–Regional Sponsored visa allows an initial stay of three years during which time the visa holder must live in a Regional or Designated Area for at least two years and work in their specified occupation for a minimum of one year.

To be eligible to apply for this subclass of visa you must be able to show the following:

- that you satisfy the basic requirements (see below)
- that you are able to pass the points test
- that you are sponsored by an eligible Australian relative living in a Designated Area or nominated by a participating State or Territory government.

To be sponsored by a relative he/she must be an Australian citizen, permanent resident or eligible New Zealand citizen who is related to you or your spouse as:

- a non-dependent child – natural, adopted or step-child
- a parent – includes adopted or step-parent
- a brother or sister – includes adopted or step-sibling
- a niece or nephew – includes adopted or step-niece/ nephew
- an aunt or uncle – includes adopted or step-aunt/uncle
- a first cousin
- a grandchild.

If you are relying on sponsorship by a person related to your spouse, partner or interdependent partner, he/she will need to be included in your application.

At the date of writing, Designated Areas are as follows:

State or Territory	Designated areas (postcodes)
Australian Capital Territory	Entire Territory
New South Wales Except Sydney, Newcastle and Wollongong	2311 to 2312
	2328 to 2333
	2336 to 2490
	2535 to 2551
	2575 to 2739
	2787 to 2898

Victoria	Entire State
Western Australia Except Perth Metropolitan Area	6042 to 6044
	6051, 6126
	6200 to 6799
South Australia	Entire State
Tasmania	Entire State
Northern Territory	Entire Territory
Queensland Except Brisbane Metropolitan Area	4019 to 4028
	4037 to 4050
	4079 to 4100
	4114, 4118
	4124 to 4150
	4158 to 4168
	4180 to 4899

At the date of writing the Regional Areas are as follows:

Regional Australia/low population growth metropolitan areas	Postcodes inclusive
New South Wales except Sydney, Newcastle, the Central Coast and Wollongong	2311 to 2312
	2328 to 2411
	2420 to 2490
	2536 to 2551
	2575 to 2594
	2618 to 2739
	2787 to 2898
Queensland except the greater Brisbane area and the Gold Coast	4124 to 4125
	4133
	4211
	4270 to 4272
	4275
	4280
	4285
	4287
	4307 to 4499
	4515
	4517 to 4519
	4522 to 4899

Victoria except Melbourne Metropolitan Area	3211 to 3334
	3340 to 3424
	3430 to 3649
	3658 to 3749
	3753
	3756
	3758
	3762
	3764
	3778 to 3781
	3783
	3797
	3799
	3810 to 3909
	3921 to 3925
	3945 to 3974
	3979
	3981 to 3996
Western Australia except Perth and surrounding areas	6041 to 6044
	6083 to 6084
	6121 to 6126
	6200 to 6799
South Australia	Entire State
Tasmania	Entire State
Northern Territory	Entire Territory

Once you have lived in Regional Australia or a Designated Area for at least two years and are able to show evidence that you have been employed for a minimum of 12 months, you are eligible to apply for permanent residence through a range of categories of regional visa which should be checked with the Department of Immigration and Citizenship at the time of application.

Basic requirements

To be eligible to apply for a Skilled–Regional Sponsored visa you must meet the following criteria:

◆ speak competent English

◆ be under 45 years of age at the time of application

◆ have an occupation that is listed on the Skilled Occupations list (please refer to Appendix 1, where a detailed version of this document is listed)

◆ have obtained a successful outcome of your skills assessment from the relevant assessing authority in Australia

◆ have at least 12 to 24 months' recent work experience depending on your occupation

◆ have secured sponsorship from a relevant State/ Territory Authority, or have obtained sponsorship from a relative as detailed above.

STATE / TERRITORY SPONSORSHIP

All applicants are required to hold sponsorship from an appropriate authority of a State/Territory government. The relevant State/Territory will advise the DIAC of the approved sponsorship when it is given. Alternatively the applicant can forward the authorised Form 1224 with the application form 1276.

Each State/Territory government has their own sponsor-ship guidelines in line with their own particular employment and economic needs. Information pertaining to employment, housing, schools and other services in the regions in which you are interested can be found at *www.immi.gov.au/migration/skilled/sir.htm.*

Skilled–Regional Sponsored applicants must be aware that sponsorship by a State/Territory government does *not* mean any of the following.

◆ Your Skilled Regional Sponsored (SRS) visa will be automatically granted. Applicants will be assessed against the legal requirement in place and only if all criteria are met will a visa be granted.

◆ Employment will be arranged by the relevant State/ Territory government who sponsors you. Individuals should make every effort to contact potential employers and arrange interviews in their chosen location.

◆ You will be granted permanent residency at the expiry of your visa. To apply for permanent residency you must have abided by all conditions of your SRS visa and lodge an application under one of the following categories:
  – Regional Sponsored Migration scheme (RSMS)
  – General Skilled Permanent category
  – Sponsored Business Owner category.

Details of theses categories can be found in other chapters.

8

Visas through Business

The Business Skills visa class of Australia's migration programme encourages successful business people to settle permanently in Australia and develop new or existing businesses. Business owners, senior executives and investors can apply for a visa under the Business Skills category.

On 1 March 2003 a two-stage process was introduced. Business migrants will be granted a Business Skills (Provisional) visa for four years and, after establishing the requisite level of business or maintaining their eligible investment, they are eligible to make an application for permanent residence.

An option for permanent residence will still be available for high-calibre business migrants sponsored by State/ Territory governments. This is known as the Business Talent visa.

THE BUSINESS SKILLS PROGRAM

The Business Skills Program is divided into four categories:

- Business owners: for owners or part-owners of a business

- Senior executives: for senior executive employees of major businesses

- Investor: for investors/business people willing to invest in Australia

- Business talent: for high-calibre business people who have sponsorship from a State/Territory government.

In addition, the Business Skills Program has two categories for persons who are in Australia on temporary visas, other than the Business Skills (Provisional) visa:

- established business in Australia (EBA): for people temporarily in Australia who are owners or part-owners of a business

- regional established business in Australia (REBA): for people temporarily in Australia who are owners or part-owners of a business in a designated area of Australia.

STATE/TERRITORY GOVERNMENT SPONSORSHIP

If an Australian State or Territory government business agency wants to encourage a particular business or business person to Australia, it can offer to sponsor the applicant.

You may obtain sponsorship in the Business Owner, Senior Executive and Investor categories. You must obtain sponsorship in the Business Talent and Regional Established Business in Australia (REBA) categories.

If you obtain State or Territory government sponsorship, you are entitled to be considered against lower threshold criteria.

State and Territory governments have their own criteria for deciding whom they will sponsor. The State or Territory government business development agency provide information on sponsorship and this can be obtained by visiting their websites.

- Australian Capital Territory – Office of Multicultural Affairs
- New South Wales – Business Migrant Information and Referral Service
- Northern Territory – Department of Industries and Business
- Queensland – Business Migration
- South Australia – Business and Skilled Migration
- Tasmania – Trade, Marketing and Major Events
- Victoria – Business Migration, Industry Victoria
- Western Australia – Small Business Development Corporation

BUSINESS OWNER CATEGORY

You must first apply for a Business Owner (Provisional) visa. If you are successful, you will be granted a visa for a period of four years.

Providing you have successfully operated a business in Australia for at least two years and you continue to hold a valid Business Skills (Provisional) visa, you will be eligible to apply for a permanent Business Owner (Residence) visa (permanent residence). You must apply in Australia.

If an applicant has sponsorship from a State or Territory government and applies under the State/Territory Sponsored Business Owner (Provisional) or (Residence) visa, they are considered against lower threshold criteria.

To make an application for the Business Owner (Provisional) visa, business owners will need to show that they fulfil the following criteria.

If unsponsored
- have an overall successful business career
- have an ownership interest of at least 10% in a business
- have significant net assets in business
- have significant business and personal assets
- have sufficient net assets to settle in Australia
- have achieved a significant annual turnover in their business
- have direct and continuous management role in overseas business
- have a commitment to maintain an ownership interest in a business in Australia and direct and continuous involvement in management of that business
- have no history of unacceptable business activities
- be less than 45 years old
- have vocational English.

If sponsored

- ◆ be sponsored by a State or Territory government
- ◆ have an overall successful business career
- ◆ have significant business and personal assets
- ◆ have achieved a significant annual turnover in their business or have continuous employment record at senior level for at least four years
- ◆ have sufficient net assets to settle in Australia
- ◆ have direct and continuous management role in overseas business
- ◆ have a commitment to maintain an ownership interest in a business in Australia and direct and continuous involvement in management of that business
- ◆ have no history of unacceptable business activities
- ◆ be less than 55 years old unless exceptional circumstances exist.

To make an application for the Business Owner (Residence) visa, business owners will need to show that they fulfil the following criteria.

If unsponsored

- ◆ hold any of the Business Skills (Provisional) visas
- ◆ have an ownership interest in one or more actively operating main business(es) for at least two years
- ◆ be involved in strategic management of the business(es)
- ◆ employ at least two Australian citizens or permanent resident employees who are not family members
- ◆ have substantial business and personal assets
- ◆ have substantial net assets in business
- ◆ have achieved a significant annual turnover in their business
- ◆ have no history of unacceptable business activities

- have been in Australia as the holder of a qualifying visa for at least one year in the last two years.

If sponsored
- be sponsored by a State or Territory government
- hold any of the Business Skills (Provisional) visas or a Temporary Business (Long Stay) Independent Executive visa
- have an ownership interest in one or more actively operating main business(es) for at least two years
- be involved in strategic management of the business
- have substantial net assets in business or have substantial net business and personal assets or employ at least one Australian citizen or permanent resident – employee who is not a family member (you must satisfy two out of these three points unless you are able to provide a waiver from the sponsoring State/Territory)
- have achieved a significant annual turnover in their business
- have no history of unacceptable business activities
- have been in Australia as the holder of a qualifying visa for at least one year in the last two years.

SENIOR EXECUTIVE CATEGORY

To make an application for the Senior Executive (Provisional) visa, senior executives will need to show that they meet the following requirements.

If unsponsored
- have an overall successful business career
- be employed in one of the top three levels of management of a major business
- have significant business and personal assets

- have sufficient net assets to settle in Australia
- have a commitment to maintain an ownership interest in a business in Australia and direct and continuous involvement in management of that business
- have no history of unacceptable business activities
- be less than 45 years old
- have vocational English.

If sponsored
- be sponsored by a State or Territory government
- have an overall successful business career
- be employed in one of the top three levels of management of a major business
- have significant business and personal assets
- have sufficient net assets to settle in Australia
- have a commitment to maintain an ownership interest in a business in Australia and direct and continuous involvement in management of that business
- be less than 55 years old unless exceptional circumstances exist.

INVESTOR CATEGORY

This section contains information on who can apply for migration to Australia under the Investor category (unsponsored or sponsored). To make an application for the Investor (Provisional) visa, investors will need to show that they meet the following requirements.

If unsponsored
- have a successful record of business or investment management
- be willing to make a significant investment in a government-approved Designated Investment for four years

- have significant business and personal assets
- have sufficient net assets to settle in Australia
- have no history of unacceptable business activities
- be less than 45 years old
- have vocational English.

If sponsored

- be sponsored by a State or Territory government and intend to live in that State or Territory for a minimum of two years
- have a successful record of business or investment management
- be willing to make a significant investment in a government approved Designated Investment for four years
- have significant business and personal assets
- have sufficient net assets to settle in Australia
- have no history of unacceptable business activities
- be less than 55 years old, unless exceptional circumstances exist.

To make an application for the Investor (Residence) visa, investors will need to show that they meet the following requirements.

If unsponsored

- hold an Investor (Provisional) visa;
- have maintained their designated investments for the minimum four years
- have been in Australia as the holder of a qualifying visa for at least two years in the last four years.

If sponsored

- be sponsored by a State or Territory government
- hold a State/Territory Sponsored Investor (Provisional) visa
- have maintained their designated investments for the minimum four years
- have been resident in the sponsoring State or Territory as the holder of a qualifying visa for at least two years in the last four years.

BUSINESS TALENT CATEGORY

High-calibre business persons may apply for direct permanent residence in the first instance. If you are successful you will be granted a permanent visa.

To make an application for the Business Talent visa, business people will need to show that they:

- are sponsored by a State or Territory government
- have an overall successful business career
- have significant net assets in business
- have significant business and personal assets
- have achieved a significant annual turnover in their business
- have a commitment to maintain an ownership interest in a business in Australia and direct and continuous involvement in management of that business
- have no history of unacceptable business activities
- be less than 55 years old unless exceptional circumstances exist.

BUSINESS OWNER VISA

You must be able to demonstrate that you have had a

successful business career. This includes holding at least 10% ownership in a business, being involved in the strategic management of the business, have net assets of at least A$200,000 if you are unsponsored and A$100,000 if you are sponsored in two of the last four fiscal years. You must notify an Australian State or Territory government business development agency of your intention to engage in business in Australia and score at least 105 points in the Business Owners' points test. Please note that any points described in this outline are relevant at the date of publication; for up-to-date information on the points contact your nearest Australian consulate or mission.

All applicants for a Business Skills visa have to meet specific obligations after their arrival in Australia and must sign a declaration stating that they will adhere to these standards. In signing this form they acknowledge that if they do not make genuine efforts to participate in business within three years of the visa being granted (whether the visa was issued in or out of Australia) then DIAC has the right to cancel that visa and the visas of their family.

The obligations for a Business Owner are that they will obtain a substantial ownership interest in an eligible business in Australia; this business may be new or existing as long as it does one or more of the following:

♦ creates international market links, maintains or increases employment in Australia

- exports Australian-made goods or services or produces goods that would otherwise be imported

- improves or introduces new technology to Australia and improves commercial activity and competitiveness within sectors of the Australian economy.

Business Owners must keep DIAC informed of their current address for three years and participate in DIAC's monitoring surveys.

Applications can be made for this category from either outside or inside Australia.

Business Owner self-test

Age		**Points**
Your age at the time of application:	20–29	20
	30–44	30
	45–49	25
	50–54	10
	under 20	0
	over 55	0

Language ability

Language ability at decision:

Better than functional	30
Functional English	20
Bilingual in non-English languages	10
Limited English	10
No English	0

Turnover

If your main business(es) had an annual turnover, in two	A$5,000,000 +	60
	A$3,000,000 +	55

of the last four fiscal years before your application, of:	A$1,500,000 +	50
	A$750,000 +	40
	A$,500,000 +	35
	less than A$500,000	0

Labour costs

If your main business(es) had annual costs, in two of the last four fiscal years before your application, of:	minimum A$500,000	10
	minimum A$250,000	5
	less than A$250,000	0

Total assets

If your main business(es) had total assets, in two of the last four fiscal years before your application, of:	minimum A$1,500,000	10
	minimum A$,750,000	5
	less than A$,750,000	0

Net assets at decision

If your (or your spouse's) net assets, available for transfer to Australia within two years are:	minimum A$2,500,000	15
	minimum A$1,500,000	10
	minimum A$,500,000	5
	less than A$,500,000	0

Sponsorship

| If you are sponsored by an authorised Australian State/ Territory development agency | | 15 |

SENIOR EXECUTIVE CATEGORY

To be eligible for this category you must be able to demonstrate that you have a successful career. This includes being able to show that you were employed in one of the top three levels of management in a major business with a turnover of A$50,000,000 if you are not sponsored and A\$10,000,000 if you are sponsored by an Australian state, and that your responsibilities included strategic policy development affecting a major component or wide range of operations of that business.

You must also show that you intend to engage in business as a substantial owner in an Australian company and have notified an Australian State/Territory government business agency (note that an approved Form 927 from an above-named agency must be submitted with your application and that you must also complete Form 1137 Business Skills Profile). You must score at least 105 points on the Senior Executive Category points test.

All applicants for a Business Skills visa have to meet specific obligations after their arrival in Australia and must sign a declaration stating that they will adhere to these standards. In signing this form they acknowledge that if they do not make genuine efforts to participate in business within three years of the visa being granted (whether the visa was issued in or out of Australia), then DIAC has the right to cancel that visa and the visas of their family.

The obligations for a Senior Executive are the following.

- ◆ They will obtain a substantial ownership interest in an eligible business in Australia. This business may be new or existing as long as it does one or more of the following:
  - creates international market links
  - maintains or increases employment in Australia

- exports Australian-made goods or services or produces goods that would otherwise be imported
- improves or introduces new technology to Australia
- improves commercial activity and competitiveness within sectors of the Australian economy.

◆ They will keep DIAC informed of their current address for three years.

◆ They will participate in DIAC's monitoring surveys.

Applications for this category can be made from either outside or inside Australia.

Senior Executive self-test

Age		Points
Your age at the time of application:	20–29	20
	30–44	30
	45–49	25
	50–54	10
	under 20	0
	over 55	0

Language ability

Language ability at decision:

Better than functional	30
Functional English	20
Bilingual in non-English languages	10
Limited English	10
No English	0

Business attributes

If the major business which has employed you has had, in two of	If unsponsored A$50,000,000 +	65

the last four fiscal years	If sponsored	
before your application, an	A$10,000,000 +	65
annual turnover of:		

Net assets

If your (or your spouse's) net	minimum $2,500,000	15
assets, available for transfer to	minimum $1,500,000	10
Australia within two years are:	minimum $500,000	
	less than $500,000	0

ESTABLISHED BUSINESS IN AUSTRALIA CATEGORY

Business people who establish a business in Australia can apply to migrate under the Established Business in Australia category only while they are in Australia with a temporary visa other than a bridging visa or a criminal justice visa. They will need to show that they have had at least 10% ownership in an Australian business, for at least 18 months prior to lodging their application.

You must be able to show that:

- you hold a substantive visa – that is, a visitor, student or temporary resident visa – at the time of application

- you have been in Australia for a minimum of nine months in the 12 months before the date of application

- you have held an ownership interest of at least 10% in one or more main businesses in Australia for at least 18 months immediately prior your application

- you have been responsible for the strategic management of the business(es)

- you, or you and your spouse, hold significant assets in Australia

- you score 105 points in the Established Business in Australia category points test.

All applicants for a Business Skills visa have to meet specific obligations after their arrival in Australia and must sign a declaration stating that they will adhere to these standards.

The obligations of owners of an Established Business in Australia are that they:

- intend to maintain their ownership interest in an eligible business in Australia

- keep DIAC informed of their current address for three years

- participate in DIAC's monitoring surveys.

Applications can be made for this category only from inside Australia.

Established Business in Australia self-test

Age		Points
Your age at the time of application:	20–29	20
	30–44	30
	45–49	25
	50–54	10
	under 20	0
	over 55	0

Language ability

Language ability at decision:

Better than functional	30
Functional English	20
Bilingual in non-English languages	10
Limited English	10
No English	0

Business attributes

If for one year prior to application your main business(es): 60
– employed three full time (or equivalent) Australian
permanent residents (who are non-family members), and
– had a minimum annual turnover of A$200,000 or had
exports of minimum A$100,000 a year.

Net assets

If your (or your spouse's) net	minimum A$2,500,000	15
assets, available for transfer to	minimum A$1,500,000	10
Australia within two years are:	minimum A$,500,000	5
	less than A$,500,000	0

REGIONAL ESTABLISHED BUSINESS IN AUSTRALIA CATEGORY

To apply for this category you must:

♦ show that at the time of application that you hold a long-stay business visa

♦ have been a temporary resident in Australia for a minimum of 12 out the last 24 months before you applied for the visa

♦ have had a successful business career.

♦ have held at least a 10% ownership interest in one or more main businesses in a designated area in Australia, for at least two years immediately prior to your application and that you continue to have an interest of this kind

- show that within this time-frame the business(es) have had a turnover of at least $200,000 or they export at least $100,000

- show that you, or you and your spouse, hold net assets of A$200,000 and the net assets of your main business(es) are no less than A$75,000 for the 24 months prior to the application

- show that you have been involved in the strategic management of the business(es) for the two years before you applied

- have been sponsored by a State or Territory government business agency

- have scored a minimum of 105 points in the Established Regional Business in Australia points test

- have completed a Business Skills Profile form 1138.

All applicants for a Business Skills visa have to meet specific obligations after their arrival in Australia and must sign a declaration stating that they will adhere to these standards.

The obligations of owners of a Regional Established Business in Australia are that they:

- intend to maintain their ownership interest in an eligible business in Australia

- keep DIAC informed of their current address for three years

- participate in DIAC's monitoring surveys.

Applications can be made for this category only from inside Australia.

Regional Established Business self-test

Age		Points
Your age at the time of application:	20–29	20
	30–44	30
	45–49	25
	50–54	10
	under 20	0
	over 55	0

Language ability
Language ability at decision:

Better than functional	30
Functional English	20
Bilingual in non-English languages	10
Limited English	10
No English	0

Business attributes
If for the two years prior to application your main business(es) employed:
- three full-time (or equivalent) Australian permanent residents, citizens or eligible New Zealand citizens (who are not family members) 60
- at least two full-time (or equivalent) Australian permanent residents, citizens or eligible New Zealand citizens (who are not family members) 40

Net assets

If your (or your spouse's) net assets, available for transfer to Australia within two years are:		
	minimum A$2,500,000	15
	minimum A$1,500,000	10
	minimum A$,500,000	5
	less than A$,500,000	0

Points

Sponsorship
Sponsored by a State or Territory Government
business agency   15

INVESTMENT LINKED CATEGORY

For this category:

◆ you must show that you have a successful record of
business or investment activities with at least three
years' experience in actively managing a qualifying
business(es) or investment(s) and that one out of the
past five fiscal years you have maintained direct and
continual involvement in either managing a business
with at least 10% ownership interest or managing
eligible investments of at least A$1,000,000

◆ you, or you and your spouse, must have held for the
two fiscal years before applying for the visa net assets
that are worth 50% more than the amount you intend
to invest in a Designated Investment in Australia

◆ you must have a genuine commitment to maintain a
substantial investment in a Government-approved
Designated Investment for a minimum of three years

◆ you must complete a Business Skills Profile form 1139

◆ you must score a minimum of 105 points in the
Investor Points test.

All applicants for a Business Skills visa have to meet
specific obligations after their arrival in Australia and
must sign a declaration stating that they will adhere to
these standards.

The obligations of owners of a Regional Established Business in Australia are that they will:

- maintain their investment or business activities in Australia after the three-year term of their investment expires

- keep DIAC informed of their current address for three years

- participate in DIAC's monitoring surveys

- have their visa cancelled if they withdraw the designated investment before the three-year period is completed.

Applications can be made for this category from either outside or inside Australia.

Investment Linked self-test

Age		Points
Your age at the time of application:	20–29	20
	30–44	30
	45–49	25
	50–54	10
	under 20	0
	over 55	0

Language ability
Language ability at decision:

Better than functional	30
Functional English	20
Bilingual in non-English languages	10
Limited English	10
No English	0

Points

Business (Investment) attributes

If you have deposited, for a	Minimum A$2,000,000	80
minimum three year term, a	Minimum A$1,500,000	70
designated investment of:	Minimum A$1,000,000	65
	Minimum A$750,000	60

APPLICATION COST AND CHARGES

As application charges can change without notice, it is best to check with any Australian mission or DIAC office for the latest figures. All fees and charges are normally stated in Australian dollars, so if you are applying within Australia by mail the preferred method of payment is money order, bank cheque or credit card. If you are applying within Australia in person the preferred method of payment is by debit or credit card. If you are applying outside of Australia the mission can inform you of what payment method to use and what the cost would be in your relevant currency.

Payment normally occurs via instalments. The first application charge covers you and your family unit – it is important to note that this charge is non-refundable regardless of the outcome of your visa. The second instalment is for those who are assessed as not having functional English. There is a cost for you and additional costs for any other candidates on your application. This payment covers the cost of English tuition in Australia to achieve a functional English level. Please note that this second instalment must be paid in full before your visa will be granted.

As part of your application you may also be required to pay for a medical examination for each of your family members included in the assessment. Additional costs will arise within the application process so be aware that you will need to pay for these; they may include character clearances from authorities and certified translations of some documents.

Dependants

Your application may cover your family unit. This includes you and your spouse and any dependants. Your spouse is defined as the person that you live with as husband and wife, either legally married or in common law as a *de facto* relationship. Dependent children are defined as under the age of 18 who are not married or in a *de facto* relationship or engaged to be married. They may be natural, adopted or a step-child. Children aged 18 or over should apply separately unless you can prove that they are substantially reliant on you for financial support and have been for some time for their basic needs of food, shelter and clothing.

(9)

Child Migration

Child migration is migration to Australia as the dependent child, orphan relative or adopted child of an Australian citizen, Australian permanent resident or eligible New Zealand citizen.

Within all of the following categories the child must be sponsored by an Australian citizen, Australian permanent resident or eligible New Zealand citizen.

CHILD CATEGORY

The child category is for the natural, adopted or step-child of a sponsor. Where a child was adopted after the sponsor became a permanent resident, they should apply under the Adopted Child category.

Please note that a child can be granted a permanent child visa based on a step-relationship only if the child's natural or adopted parent is no longer the spouse of the step-parent and that the step-parent has been granted legal responsibility for the child by a court.

ORPHAN RELATIVE CATEGORY

The Orphan Relative category is for a child under 18 years of age who has no parent to care for them.

ADOPTION CATEGORY

This category is for a child under 18 years of age who has been adopted or is in the process of being adopted by their sponsor.

The adoption must be supported by a State or Territory welfare authority, unless the adoptive parent has been resident for a minimum period of 12 months at the time the migration application is lodged.

The adoptive parent must be able to demonstrate that their residence overseas was not contrived for the purpose of bypassing the requirements concerning entry of the adopted child.

DEPENDENT CHILD (TEMPORARY) CATEGORY

This category is for the natural, adopted or step-child of the holder of a Provisional Partner visa.

The Dependent Child visa is a provisional visa which allows the dependent child of the holder of a provisional partner visa to travel to or remain in Australia for the same period as their parent. Once this visa has been granted the holder can apply to be included in their parent's Permanent Partner visa application.

10

Other Family Migration

Other Family Migration is defined as migration to Australia on the basis of being an aged dependent relative, remaining relative or the carer of an Australian citizen, Australian permanent resident or eligible New Zealand citizen. Within each of the Other Family Migration categories you must be sponsored by an Australian citizen, Australian permanent resident or eligible New Zealand citizen.

AGED DEPENDENT RELATIVE
Those who can apply under this category are people who are a single, widowed or divorced aged person who is dependent on a relative who lives in Australia (see below for the definition of a 'relative').

REMAINING RELATIVE

Those who can apply under this category are the brother, sister or child (or step-relative the same) of a person in Australia, who, if they did not migrate to Australia, would otherwise be left on their own overseas.

CARER

Those who can apply under the Carer category are people who are willing and able to give substantial and continual assistance to an Australian relative (or a member of their family) who has a medical condition causing physical, intellectual or sensory impairment of their ability to attend to the practical aspects of daily life.

Relatives include child, parent, sibling, grandparent, grandchild, uncle, aunt, niece or nephew (or step-relative the same).

Part Three
Living in Australia

11

Employment

The Australian labour market is very competitive and it may take time to find employment. It is suggested that you start to plan your employment before you arrive in Australia. How long it takes to find a position will depend on your skills and qualifications, recognition of them by the relevant bodies (see p. 142), which part of Australia you live or want to live in, the demand for your area of expertise and economic conditions at the time. If you work in health, trades or accounting, your skills at the time of writing this book would be welcomed in the southern and particularly, the eastern regions. With the development of wind-farms and wineries, and millions being invested by Kimberly Clark, the paper giant, and the Anchor bottle factory, skilled migrants are required.

CURRICULUM VITAE

You will need an impeccably presented CV of approximately two pages, with full details of your educational qualifications and employment history. Also include your contact details, address, phone number and email, and a brief personal history, e.g. marital status, hobbies and interests. Make copies of all birth, marriage and educational certificates, passport, degrees, diplomas, references and any other relevant paper work. *Never post your original documents*, always send copies. Usually an application for a position requires you initially, to apply in writing. You will need to write a covering letter indicating the position you are applying for, why you want the position and details of your relevant skills, experience and qualifications.

Some of the applicants will be interviewed, often by more than one person, and then there is usually a delay of a few weeks before you are advised of the outcome of your application. It is advisable to apply for as many positions as possible to increase your chances of securing a position.

FINDING WORK

'Positions Vacant' and job vacancy advertisements are listed in the classified section of the newspapers, usually on Wednesdays and Saturdays. Advertisements for positions through private employment agencies will also be found there or agencies may be contacted through the Internet employment boards or the *Yellow Pages* of the telephone directory. Look under 'Employment Services' and 'Employment – Labour Hire Contractors'. Agencies generally find you a job and charge your new employer the fee. Labour hire agencies pay you and supply your services to another company.

Online job seekers, employment and recruitment

Job Boards usually offer a range of services, including thousands of job opportunities, CV storage, career resources, employment and market information and a direct link to business websites. Be aware that some old positions may be re-advertised by agencies and search options may be limited in the executive listings.

For more information on employment opportunities contact the following Executive Recruitment Agencies:

http://www.employmentguide.com.au/Executive-recruit ment.htm
or
www.michaelpage.com.au: Michael Page, support to executive, accountancy
www.kmpg.com.au: KPMG, middle–senior management & executive
www.tannermenzies.com: Tanner Menzies, middle to executive
www.acpeople.com.au: students and recent graduates
www.employment.byron.com.au: one of the first job search websites.

The Australian Jobs & Employment Review is a regularly updated online fact site:
Email: *news@employmentguide.com.au*

Other websites worth checking are:

http://www.seek.com.au: a highly regarded site with approximately 65,000 jobs and *www.employmentguide.com.au/Job-boards.htm*

Other associated services:

www.careerone.com.au has recently been revamped, with 'News & Views' business updates and associated services

www.mycareer.com.au: comprehensive recruitment as above

www.jobnet.com.au: specifically IT profession

www.jobsearch.gov.au: government-based employment

www.jobsguide.com.au: positions outside the cities

www.thewest.com.au: employment in Perth and Western Australia

www.mine4jobs.com.au: mining industry

www.austrade.gov.au: government export/trade jobs

www.traveljobs.com.au: travel industry

Direct contact

Direct contact is a useful way of obtaining work. Approach a company you would like to work for, in person, by phone or letter and put a proposal to them. Speak to everyone around you, your professional and daily contacts, such as your lawyer, doctor, neighbour, insurance or real estate agent, about the job you want. It is often a good idea to join community groups, such as Rotary, or the Lions Clubs, your children's school committees or local Chamber of Commerce for networking opportunities. *www.bni.com.au* may be a useful contact for breakfast referral meetings.

Useful online information

Researching labour market information will help you find out what is available in the area you want to live. The following sites will tell you what is available in different cities, states or territories:

http://www.myfuture.edu.au/
- labour market information
- industry information
- occupation information

www.workplace.gov.au/
- migrants and the labour market
- state and regional information

Skills or experience in areas or regions lacking skilled labour will assist you in finding a job more quickly. The two sites mentioned above will provide you with the following information:

- current Migration Occupations in Demand List (MODL)
- skill shortages
- jobs with good prospects
- where the jobs are.

Migrants who are subject to the two-year waiting period have access to free Job Matching services through the Job Network. If you meet the criteria, this is a facility that will put you in touch with private, community and government organisations contracted by the Commonwealth Government to help facilitate employment.

For more information visit the website, *www.centrelink. gov.au* or contact your nearest Centrelink office. Addresses and phone numbers can be found in the *White Pages* telephone directory.

The Department of Employment and Workplace Relations (DEWR) has a useful website, which provides information on jobs, online services, careers, training and working conditions. For more information the website is *www.workplace.gov.au*

Qualifications, skills and additional training
Qualifications and skills may need to be recognised by the appropriate Australian authority, or membership required by a professional or industrial association. You need to be aware of these details before making your move. **Additional training** or a bridging course may also be required.

Find out more on the following websites:

◆ National Office of Overseas Skills Recognition (NOOSR) for recognition of qualification and skills and bridging for Overseas–trained professionals *www.aei.dest.gov.au/AEI/qualificationsrecognition*

◆ *www.teachingaustralia.edu.au*: teachers

◆ *www.aqf.edu.au*: Australia Qualifications Framework

◆ Trades Recognition Australia (TRA) for engineering, catering, electrical, and construction. *www.gov.au/tra* *www.workplace.gov.au/workplace/individual/migrant*

www.australia-migration.com/page/trades_TRA

◆ Bridging for Overseas-Trained Professionals Loan Scheme (BOTPLS), replaced by Fee-Help. *www.goingtouni/gov.au/main/quickfind/international students*

Tertiary qualifications also need to be recognised in Australia by the National Office of Overseas Skills Recognition (NOOSR) and for more information visit the website *www.dest.gov.au/noosr/brgcourses.htm*

Other useful addresses on the Internet are:

◆ *www.jobsearch.gov.au*
◆ *www.jobsguide.com.au* (Rural Press Limited – regional Australia)
◆ *www.careerone.com.au* (News Limited)
◆ *www.mycareer.com.au/jobseeker* (Fairfax)
◆ *www.seek.com.au/*
◆ *www.australia.gov.au/365*
◆ *www.liveinaustralia.com/home/employment_in_ australia.asp*

Tradesmen – qualifications
Tradesmen can have their qualifications tested nationally either before arrival or once you are settled in Australia. The tests are standard thoughout Australia and organised nationally by Trades Recognition Australia, TRA, part of the Commonwealth Department of Employment, Workplace Relations and Small Business. You will need to provide detailed information regarding your general education, technical or vocational education and work

experience. References from employers covering period of time employed, detailed descriptions of the work under-taken, and employment classification are very important, and the more information you can provide regarding your background the better your employment prospects. To access the application form, go to the Australian Work-place website *www.workplace.gov.au*

The Head Office postal address is:

Trades Recognition Australia
Department of Employment and Workplace Relations
GPO Box 9879
Melbourne VIC 3001
Tel: 1300 360 992 or 03 9954 2537
Fax: 03 9954 2588
artcenquiries@dewr.gov.au

WORKING IN AUSTRALIA

When you have your job you will need to open a bank account for direct payment of salary or wages, which are paid weekly, fortnightly or monthly. Tax is usually deducted at source and the record of pay (payslip) must clearly show the gross amount paid before tax.
www.oea.gov.au
http://www.en.wikipedia.org/wiki/Australian_Workplace_Agreement

Opening a bank account in the first six weeks of arrival requires only your passport as identification. After that time extra ID is required. Check out different banking institutions and accounts for variable fees, rates of interest and types of accounts.

Employment law

Employer/employee rights are mainly covered by State or Commonwealth awards, except in Victoria where federal or state industry sector awards apply. These are legally binding on the employer, cover working conditions and include overtime, minimum rates of pay, holiday, sickness and long-service leave and hours of work. Certified agreements are collective agreements made between an employer and employees or their union. An individual agreement between an employer and employee is called an Australian Workplace Agreement (AWA). By law, employees have the right to choose whether they join a union or not.

Dismissal of an employee and termination of employment are covered by law. It may pay to seek legal advice if you feel you have been unfairly dismissed.

Equal Employment Opportunity (EEO) means that anti-discrimination laws make it illegal for employees or employers to discriminate against another person based on religion, gender, race, age, marital status or pregnancy. If you have any concerns, contact the Human Rights and Equal Opportunity Commission *www.hreoc. gov.au*

Workplace harassment is behaviour by another employee that is offensive, abusive, threatening, uninvited, unwelcome and illegal.

The employer must safeguard the health and safety of employees in the workplace.

Superannuation, which most employees have, is a retirement savings programme available through the work place where every employer is required to contribute an amount equal to 9% of an employee's earnings. To check that you are receiving the correct amount and for further information contact the website for Australian Taxation Office Superannuation *www.ato.gov.au/superannuation*

Taxation

A tax file number (TFN) is required for all individuals or organisations earning income and is issued by the Australian Tax Office (ATO). This is a top priority for immigrants and can be obtained 24 hours a day, seven days a week, via the Internet with only your passport and new home address. Your new TFN will arrive by mail in ten days. Other options are to contact your local Centrelink office for an application form via the ATO website or call the TFN Helpline. Processing will take 28 days. The Tax File Number registration website is *www.ato.gov.au/individuals*

You will be required to complete a TFN Declaration form with your own TFN. An Income Tax form must be lodged each year by 31 October in the financial year (between 1 July and 30 June) that you earn income. At the end of the financial year, your employer must provide you with a Payment Summary of your annual earnings.

GST (Goods and Services Tax) of 10% is included in and payable on most items. Childcare, nursing home care, health services, most education and basic food items are exempt.

Capital gains tax applies if you make a capital gain (or profit) as a result of selling (or otherwise disposing of) certain assets.

The Tax Office website – *www.ato.gov.au* – will provide information for claiming work-related expenses, paying fringe benefit tax, and retirement and investment information.

If you operate a business you will require a number specific to your business dealings with the Australian tax office. It is recommended that you seek professional advice or contact the Australian Tax Office
www.ato.gov.au

(12)

Starting a Business

People with the skills to establish and manage a business in a competitive environment are very welcome in Australia. Women under 30 are responsible for the fastest growth in small businesses and operations based at home – utilising computer technology. If you are self-employed it is essential to develop and maintain links with other businesses/people by joining local groups – see Direct Contact, page 140 for suggestions.

IMPORTANT INFORMATION

The following list will give you an idea of the areas that you need to research when starting a small business:

◆ You need to be certain that you have the health, personal qualities and experience required to own and operate a business.

◆ Many businesses in Australia require a licence or

permit to operate. This term refers to any form of government regulation, registration, permit or approval that applies to a small business. The Business Licence and Information Centre (BLIS) creates listings of local state and federal licences relevant to your business. These may include registering the business name, choosing the structure, running a home-based business, employing staff, registering for taxation purposes, playing music in the workplace and erecting signs. BLIS website is *http://www.licence.sbdc.com.au/content/ businessdefault.html* or *http://www.licence.sbdc.com.au/ content/businessindex.html* Go to the *licence enquiry* section, select your business activity, add your business details and a list of all the areas of your business that require licensing and the relevant licences for every area – local, State and Federal – will be displayed. Or for free specific business licensing, registration and information contact *Smart*licence: website *http://bli.net.au/DIR0121/ BLI home.nsf/States/* and add QLD NSW, WA, NT, VIC or TAS depending on which State you need information on.

◆ You may also need to check with the industry association relevant to your business for the Codes of Practice – guidelines which specify business practices and standards.

◆ Next you need to research and reassure yourself that your business concept is commercially viable. A written business plan is essential at this stage with spreadsheets (available from Small Business Development Corporation (SBDC) see page 153) of the projected cash flow analysis, break-even calculations and forward budgets.

The Commonwealth Government bookstore, banks and the SBDC have available various publications which will assist you.

♦ After completing the above, finances need to be planned and arranged. Some new businesses are able to borrow funds, which means that capital can be reserved. Be very careful at this stage and make sure you have good advice. The old adage 'A fool and his money are easily parted' is as applicable in Australia as anywhere else in the world.

♦ Your accountant or professional business adviser will advise you which of the following company structures are most appropriate for your business.
  - **Sole Trader** – easy to start up a small business and the owner is liable for debts.
  - **Partnership** – a Partnership Agreement is recommended and the partners are liable for the debts.
  - **Proprietor Ltd Company (incorporated), Discretionary or Unit Trust** or a combination of any of the above.

  The decision will reflect the type of business, projected profitability, the financial status and relationships of those involved in the new venture. A common procedure is to purchase a Shelf Company for approximately A$1,100 (see Shelf Company Services in the *Yellow Pages* of the telephone directory).

♦ Your adviser will ensure your business structure meets legal requirements, that your assets are protected, your tax (including Capital Gains taxes) minimised and that your business has the flexibility for new partners or investors to become involved if required.

◆ Location and premises are vital for most businesses. Remember that parking, visibility, and plenty of floor space and passing traffic are essential for success. Familiarise yourself with the surrounding competition and businesses.

◆ Enlist professional advice for entering into the lease agreement and to ensure that your business can operate long term.

◆ Check with the local council for any by-laws, health department requirements and new roads/developments that may affect your business.

◆ Check with your accountant or the Australian Tax Office to ascertain the taxes you need to pay: personal, company, Capital Gains (on the sale of property), fringe benefits, (perks of the job, e.g. car) sales, rental, business and stamp and artist's royalties. Books need to be maintained daily and records kept for five years. For confidential tax advice contact the SBDC at the website on page 153.

◆ Register your business name. To search for business and company names, go to *www.abr.gov.au* or *www.asic.gov.au*

◆ Contact an insurance broker or a recommended agent for life and general insurance policies for partners and management. Worker's compensation insurance is compulsory for all employees, including management and directors. National Insurance Brokers Association *www.niba.com.au*

- Carefully select your staff and provide each person with a written job description. The Department of Productivity and Labour Relations and Department of Occupational Health, Safety and Welfare will advise on hours, holidays, leave, superannuation and safety. If purchasing a business, check ongoing training commitments, long-service leave and any other liabilities. *www.labourdept.gov.LK.lab_aust*

- Check as to whether you require computers or printed business documentation such as invoices, statements, receipts and payslips. Initially you may be able to use available business stationery or secretarial services.

- Decide whether your business requires vehicles. If so, what sort? Will they be leased or owned by the company? Check the taxation status, i.e. fringe benefit tax.

- Security of your premises and of cash or stock is paramount.

- Plan your marketing and advertising using data from your business plan. (Business cards, brochures, referrals, media, trade shows, vehicles, sales people and telemarketing, and direct mail are all commonly used advertising.)

- Decide what credit, terms of credit and debt services you will provide.

- Consider the communication and business technology you will use. (Photocopiers, two way radio, mobile phones, after-hours answer services and computers.)

◆ To operate a successful small business, you may require formal training to manage the accounting, marketing, staff selection, supervisory skills and inventory control. The Small Business Development Corporation, SBDC, runs 'How To Start A Business' workshops. For essential information on starting a business and relevant market intelligence, the Australian Taxation Office has publications available which can be downloaded from the website (*www.ato.gov.au*).

◆ Credit Code details and assistance for everyone providing or using credit, e.g. retailers and consumers, are available on the web site: *www.creditcode.gov.au* Also available is a free copy of the national Uniform Consumer Credit Code.

◆ *austrade.gov.au* provides information and support for potential exporters, and also information for those looking to source goods, services and investments in Australia. Also available is student, tertiary study and career information.

Other useful websites

For further assistance, the email address of the SBDC is *info@sbdc.com.au/* or go to website: *www.sbdc.com.au*.

The website for the Business Licence Information Service is *www.bli.net.au/* or phone your nearest Business Enterprise Centre.

http://www.licence.sbdc.com.au/content/linksdefault.html is a website that gives access to the following areas: small business in Western Australia, licensing and other regulatory requirements, business and domain names, taxation information, information on employing staff, selling to government and importing and exporting.

For business and domain names, the Australian Securities and Investments Commission (ASIC) website contains a national index of corporate and business names. It also has information on the rights and responsibilities of small business owners and is responsible for company registration matters. You can lodge an application online for a domain name if you are setting up a website. All tax related issues are also available on this address
www.asic.gov.au

www.austrade.gov.au provides information and support for potential exporters and also information for those looking to source goods, services and investments in Australia. Student, study and career information is also available.

13

Transport

DRIVING IN AUSTRALIA

A car is essential when living in Australia as public transport in many of the newer suburbs is virtually non-existent. Looking for a job, house or school outside the ten-mile radius of many city centres could be very difficult without a car. Air conditioning, very necessary in summer, is usually standard, and power steering is recommended for comfortable long-distance driving. If you already own a good car and want to take it to Australia, first check all the costs and make sure it will comply with Australian design rules.

Private vehicles can be prepurchased over the Internet and be ready and awaiting your arrival at the airport. Some firms offer incentives to purchase, such as savings on servicing and the opportunity to earn a referral fee for every successful referral made.

For more details, go to *www.ahg.co.au* and for Western Australia try *www.giantautos.com.au*

For shipping costs refer to *www.doreebonner.co.uk*, *www.britannia-movers.co.ltd*, *www.anglopacific.co.uk*, *http://www.karmanshipping.com*, *www.carshipping.co.uk* or Email: *moving@dbonner.co.uk, info@anglopacific.co.uk, interconti@btconnect.com, international@britannia-movers.co.uk*

For competitive quotes from different companies go to *www.uk-removal.co.uk*. Do check another company or two.

Newspapers display personal sale advertisements, show-rooms or yards where new or second-hand cars are available. For information on the best cars to buy and the warranties required by different states it is advised that you purchase car magazines, newspapers and check relevant websites.

Usually, once you have chosen the car you will need to pay registration, stamp duty and compulsory third party insurance. Every state and territory has a motorist association, which will provide purchasers (members or non-members) with a pre-sale check, insurance and roadside breakdown cover.

The Australian Automobile Association (AAA) is widely recognised by government and industry as the official voice of Australia's motorist, has 6.2 million members and represents indirectly all Australian motorists at the national and international levels. Contact details for the AAA are *http://www.aaa.asn.au* Also useful is the National Road Motorists' Association *www.nrma.com.au* Go to branch locations for your local contact, and for South Australia, the Royal Automobile Association, *www.raa.net/*

To check if anyone owes money on a second-hand car that you want to buy, with a registration from any state or territory, visit the Registrar of Encumbered Vehicles website, *www.revs.nsw. gov.au*

Rules of the road
Road rules to remember include:

◆ Australians drive on the left.

◆ Always give way to your right.

◆ Three traffic light phases (four in the UK).

◆ Keep your seat belt fastened at all times – this applies to every passenger in the car.

◆ General speed limits include: 60kph in built-up areas and 100kph – 110kph in the country depending on which State you are in.

◆ There is random breath testing for alcohol throughout the country. The safest advice is not to drink and drive but if you are stopped you will be charged and lose your licence if your blood alcohol level exceeds 0.05 per cent.

Fuel facts
Petrol prices vary from A$1.15 in South Australia to

A$1.35 per litre in the Northern Territories. Check *www.motormouth.com.au* for pump rates for Brisbane, Sunshine and Gold Coast, Sydney, Melbourne, Adelaide, Perth and South Australia. Also try: *www.fuelwatch.wa. gov.au* and *www.mynrma.com.au-petrolwatch*

Fuel is more expensive once you get out into the country and outback. Diesel and unleaded fuel are readily available and regular leaded fuel is being slowly phased out. Most service stations are self-service with automatic pumps. A wide range of credit cards is accepted at large service stations, although many of the smaller stations may accept only Visa and MasterCard. Also remember that the Australian distances are vast and that inland country towns are often very far apart. It is wise to work out the distances that you are travelling and where you are going to be able to stop and fill up to ensure that you do not run out of petrol in a very isolated part of the country.

Driving licence
Your current driver's licence is valid for three months after becoming an Australian resident. After that time you will have to apply for an Australian licence that will require you to pass a written and practical test of the road rules and have your eyes tested.

Renting a car
Car rental operators within Australia include Budget, Hertz, Avis, Alamo and Thrifty, all of which have very similar rates. Other smaller operators offer cheaper cars but you should examine the insurance and excess prices as they could make the end price higher. Most companies will rent only to drivers aged 25 or older and you will need to provide your home country's licence or an Interna-

tional licence – these are valid within Australia for a period of up to one year. Try *www.easycar.com/car-hire/links/australia* for more information.

Campervans, caravans, motorhomes and poptops

Campervans, caravans, motorhomes and poptops are an excellent way to explore Australia, as the millions of road miles, particularly outside of the cities, are relatively traffic free. A campervan, or any of the above, is easy to drive and also very cost efficient if there are more than two in your family or group, as costs to park on the many nationwide sites with facilities (basic is power and water) are minimal compared with hotel and motel rates. You are not committed to a schedule and can choose to spend a night in an establishment at your leisure. You only require your valid licence and need to remember that the vehicle is larger than normal when parking and reversing. However, you will be advised, whether you decide to rent or purchase, on any extra information you may need.

Papers usually carry advertisements, but specialist magazines like *Caravan Trader* and *Campervan & Motorhome Trader* are the best source. The choice is huge and there are many different options. You may even decide to start a coach tour business!

Using taxis

Taxis in Australia operate on a meter system except in some country towns. Fares are displayed on the meter and all drivers must also display a photo and identification card. You can stop and flag down a taxi for hire whenever you see one or, for an extra charge, book a taxi over the phone. Smoking is not permitted in many public vehicles so it is advisable to ask your driver first. Limousines are inexpensive and easily available for hire in many of the main centres. Most areas offer a special taxi service for people using a wheelchair, but it is recommended that bookings are made in advance to ensure availability.

PUBLIC TRANSPORT

Travelling by air

Air transport is provided in Australia by the three international airlines, Qantas, Virgin Blue and JetStar, who offer a similar service of internal flights on domestic networks, alongside other, smaller feeder airlines. As Australia is such a vast and empty country the only practical way to tackle long distances and extensive travel is by air. There is a range of discount fares available for international travellers – provided you book these before you leave your home country. Every town and city has an airfield, as do many individual properties in the country, while most business travel is done by air. For more information try *www.quantas.com/au, www.virginblue.com.au,* and *www.jetstar.com.au,* also *www.bugaustralia.co/transport/air, www.frog&toad.com.au* Also check out the Apex Advance Purchase Eurasian fares.

Taking a train

Trains run from one end of the nation to the other in a vast railway network, although not as comprehensively as some of the overseas railway systems. Modern air-conditioned trains operate on the outback and coastal routes. The main lines follow the east and south coast, linking the cities of Cairns, Brisbane, Sydney, Melbourne and Adelaide. Lines from Adelaide connect with the line between Sydney and Perth. If you plan to do a lot of travel by train initially, you are entitled to an 'Austrailpass'. This pass can only be purchased overseas by the holder of a foreign passport and allows unlimited travel in first or economy class on interstate or metropolitan trains nation-wide. For more information try *www.seat61.com/ australia.htm, www.countrylink.info* and *www.railaustralia. com*

Using the ferry

Ferry services offered interstate for regular travel are *The Spirit of Tasmania* which links Melbourne and Devon-port, Tasmania, and the *Seacat* which runs between Port Welshpool in Victoria and George Town in Tasmania. Sydney has her own cruise and urban ferry services, often the preferred mode of transport for commuters, that operate constantly around the harbour, while Perth also has a ferry link across the Swan River.

Travelling by coach

Long-distance coaches are usually of a high standard, with air conditioning, reclining seats and toilets on services provided by Nationwide or Countrylink Intrastate, Grey-hound Pioneer, and Interstate. A luxury coach service is available to 299 country towns, which allows travel almost anywhere in Australia. If you plan to travel by coach, discounts may be available for early booking and extensive travel. Also check what services are offered on board. See *www.greyhound.com.au* and *www.premierms.com/*

Urban transport

Urban transport networks range from good to adequate. Sydney, Melbourne, Brisbane, Adelaide and Perth all offer bus and train services. Hobart, Canberra and Darwin offer only a bus service. Contact CountryLink for the express train services around New South Wales and to Melbourne and Brisbane. Passes are available which allow unlimited stopovers and travel as far north as Cairns. The relevant websites are: *www.apta.com/links/ international/australia.cfm, www.clickforaustralia.com/ australia_ transportation_trains_bus_services.htm* and *www.sydneybuses.nsw.gov.au*

14

Education in Australia

Educational standards in Australia are amongst the highest in the world, as the Federal and State Governments are responsible for regulating and maintaining the system. The Federal Department of Education, Science and Training (DEST) is the main government body responsible for overall education policies, ensuring consistent standards throughout Australia. By minimising educational differences between States and Territories, students across the country compete equally at the levels required for entry into tertiary education.

FINDING A SCHOOL FOR YOUR CHILD

Because Australians believe access to quality education is the birthright of each child, male or female, parents and the community are closely involved in maintaining the high level of learning. Parent and teacher associations are active in every area of education from fundraising to curriculum decisions, and often even in the contribution of their skills. Consequently, the school participation rate is one of the best in the world, with more time spent at school than England, Japan and Germany. Immigrants may find the teaching system and school discipline different, as emphasis is placed on encouraging a child's interest and enthusiasm through learning by finding out, questioning, and self-discipline. Schooling is compulsory until the age of 15 in most Territories and States. Students usually leave after completing Year 10 or stay on until the end of Year 12.

Parents can choose to have their children educated in a public or private school. The public school system is owned and funded by the Government, and is usually coeducational. Public schools teach a mixture of languages through a syllabus called 'LOTE' – Language Other Than English. Although free to everyone, a small annual fee is often required to cover annual costs and extra-curricular activities, and parents are expected to pay for books, outings and uniforms. Private schools, where students pay annual fees, are usually single sex and administered by an independent or religious body. They will usually also offer a more diverse range of specialist subjects such as computing studies, science and music.

Approximately 35% of children are currently enrolled at private schools throughout Australia, and early registration of your child is recommended as competition for entry is strong and waiting lists are increasing.

To find schools in your area visit the website *www.dest. gov.au/schools/authorit.htm*

Pre-schooling, daycare, playgroups

The starting age for pre-school is three years and attendance is usually part-time with morning and afternoon sessions. Because these are privately owned, early registration is advisable, as places are often limited. Working parents may need to make enquiries for other full-time childcare arrangements. Most child minders require a licence or basic qualifications.

Infant and primary schools

Infants and primary schools group children together on the basis of age and development level. Progression to the following year is based on evaluation of the student's development during the year. Primary school subjects are based on the eight key learning areas: English, language other than English, health and physical education, maths, science, the arts, technology, society and the environment. Children are also taught about Australian culture and society, and learn that tolerance of all people of every race and background is fundamental in a happy community. Usually pupils wear school uniform, which includes a hat. Research has shown that long-term exposure to the sun can damage the skin so a policy of 'no hat – no play' is enforced.

The school timetable varies from State to State and will have three or four terms with holidays in between. Remember, there will be a lot of adjustments to make for the younger people if you are immigrating permanently. It is important to settle children into school where they can develop a routine and make new friends as quickly as possible. Careful planning is required to coincide your arrival with the start of the new school year, which runs from February to November. You will need to check with your doctor whether your child requires immunisation before going to school.

Secondary education

Secondary school education is compulsory up to age of 15, although two more years of schooling follow, which the majority of students complete. English, science and maths are compulsory during the first couple of years, with a broad range of elective subjects that the students can choose. As students progress through the school system, teachers will actively encourage them to talk through subject options and career directions with a career adviser. This is important, especially as universities require specific papers to be completed before entry into some courses. Supplementary education, in the form of correspondence papers or school on Saturday, is offered if the course that the student wants to enrol in conflicts with other papers or is not currently on offer at their school.

The relevant State (or Territory) authorities accredit all registered courses of study at secondary school. Completing the final year of study does not entitle the student to immediate entry into the university course of their choice. Places in tertiary courses are limited and competition is strong.

The International Baccalaureate

The International Baccalaureate is a programme with a high international profile and is offered during the last few years of school. This course allows the student to gain entry into a number of overseas universities and get an advanced placement in some American universities.

UNIVERSITY EDUCATION

Australian universities are regarded as amongst the best in the world and Australia is the third most popular study destination in the English-speaking world. Australia's 50 plus institutions prepare students for entry into specific professions and encompass both teaching and research. All offer a full range of academic and professional disciplines with awards ranging from diplomas to associate doctorates. Some universities have a multi-campus structure, which offers specialised courses, while others offer on-site residential accommodation, external clubs and extra-curricular activities to enhance the student lifestyle. An average degree will take from three years plus with six years for double degree with honours.

For information on admission and courses, contact the individual university (list follows) or visit the following websites:

www.dest.gov.au/tenfields, *www.dest.gov.au/highered* or *www.internationaledu.net* The website *http://studyinaus tralia.gov.au* has further information in 20 languages.

List of universities in Australia:
Adelaide University *www.adelaide.edu.au*
Australian Catholic University *www.acu.edu.au/* (six

campuses) Ballarat, Brisbane, Canberra, Melbourne, North Sydney and Strathfield

Australian Correspondence Schools *www.acs.edu.au/ distance-education.html*

Australian Defence Force Academy *www.adfa.oz.au*

Australian International Hotel School *www.adfa.oz.au/*

Australian National University *www.anu.edu.au*

Avondale, Degrees with a Christian focus *www.avondale.edu.au*

Barton Institute of Technical and Further Education (TAFE)

Bedford Business College

Bond University

Canberra College of Theology

Central Queensland University

Charles Sturt University *www.csu.edu.au*

Claremont College

Collaborative Information Technology Research Institute

Curtin University of Technology, Western Australia

Deakin University

Edith Cowan University

Flinders University

Griffith University

James Cook University

La Trobe University

Macquarie University *www.mq.edu.au*

Monash University

Monash Mt Eliza Business School

Murdoch University

Northern Territory University

Open Learning University

Queen's College

Queensland International Heritage College
Queensland University of Technology
Royal Melbourne Institute of Technology
Southern Cross University *www.scu.edu.au*
Swinburne University of Technology
Sydney Institute of Technology
School of Mines and Industries Ballarat
University of Adelaide
University of Ballarat
University of Canberra *www.canberra.edu.au*
University of New England *www.une.edu.au*
University of New South Wales
University of Newcastle
University of Notre Dame Australia
University of Queensland
University of South Australia
University of Southern Queensland
University of Sydney
University of Tasmania
University of Technology, Sydney
University of Western Australia
University of Western Sydney, Hawkesbury
University of Western Sydney, Macarthur
University of Western Sydney, Nepean
University of Wollongong
Victoria University of Technology

For further information you may find the following websites useful:

www.idp.com an independent non-profit organisation which represents all aspects of Australian learning

www.australiangraduate.com/universities.htm
www.edna.edu.au/edna
www.dest.gov.au/highered/courses.htm
www.uac.edu.au (the Universities Admission Centre website).

There is a student loan system for those who meet the
requirements, or a student may choose to pay fees, which
are less than those of many other countries. Time payment
for books and union fees is also available to those who
qualify. For further details contact the Higher Education
Contribution Scheme (HECS) website, *www.hecs.gov.au*

CAREER AND VOCATIONAL TRAINING
Adult and community education courses facilitate lifelong
learning, are inexpensive, easily accessible and well
adapted to the requirements of adults. For further
information contact the website, *www.edna.edu.au/edna/*

There are public and private education services provided
in this sector:

♦ TAFE (Technical and Further Education is regulated
by the Government) *www.tafenew.edu.au*

♦ ACPET (the Australian Council of Private Education
and Training) *www.acpet.edu.au*

These courses have a practical focus towards the career
that the student is aiming for. Fees are charged with costs
varying between courses, tertiary institutes and States.
Most courses offer a diploma or associate diploma level
and a few are offered as degrees.

The Australian Qualifications Framework

Australian Qualifications Framework (AQF) is a government-supported, nationwide system of qualifications recognised by some countries worldwide. For more information check the website *www.aqf.edu.au* which includes a guide to studying in Australia in 18 community languages.

Recognition of Qualificatioins

Recognition of Qualifications is a national body responsible for recognising overseas and Australia qualifications. See the Australian Education Awards and educational system website, *www.immi.gov.au/ settle/education/qualifications.htm*

The Federal Department of Education, Training and Youth Affairs (DETYA) is responsible overall in Australia for a national education policy and consistency of standards.

CHILDCARE SERVICES

Childcare services must be licensed and are available for babies from birth to nursery, through early childhood and for toddlers up to three years. After-school and holiday care is also available for primary school children up to 12 years of age. Different types of childcare are: long day care centres, family day care centres, occasional care, outside school hours care, vacation care services, playgroups, multifunctional children's services and mobile children's services and toy libraries. Some parents are able to claim financial assistance towards childcare costs. For more information contact the National Childcare Accreditation Council, *www.ncac.gov.au*

FINANCIAL ASSISTANCE

Educational scholarships are available. Look for information on the following websites:

www.dest.gov.au/highered/scholarships.htm (Education Network Australia's Link to scholarship sites).

www.hecs.gov.au/links.htm (Department of Training and Youth Affairs Information on Scholarships).

Assistance for Children with Special Needs can be obtained through local schools who will put you in touch with the State or Territory education department where a full range of options is available for a child requiring special educational facilities. The Department of Human Services (DHS) has developed a new service for the above. Go to *www.dhs.state.ri.us/famchild/dchspec.htm* Parents of adolescents who require help can contact the Reach Out! Service which offers advice for both parents and teenagers: *www.reachout.com.au*.

The Source is a youth information website provided by the Commonwealth Government: *www.thesource.gov.au*. More information is available from *www.immi.gov.au/settle/youth*.

Depending on the State that you choose to live in, you will need to check all of the above information to see what is applicable to your particular visa and circumstances.

$$\left(15\right)$$

Housing

'Where shall I live?' will be your main question if you are immigrating permanently. Climate has to be one of the first considerations. Australia, the world's smallest continent or the biggest island, offers a wide choice of weather, ranging from tropics, rain forests and stunning untouched coastlines in the far north, to the interior desert, and down to the cooler more temperate Mediterranean appearance of the south coast, through to the Alps in the east where skiers enjoy superb snow conditions. The new immigrant looking for a healthy and different lifestyle has a variety of climatic regions where a desirable environment and community will suit the requirements of any family.

The monsoon belt, which includes Darwin and Cairns, lies in the tropical zone north of the Tropic of Capricorn and covers nearly 40% of Australia. This area has only two seasons: the 'dry' from April to November with warm days, clear blue skies and cool nights and the 'wet' which falls between December and March. The highest rainfall on the Great Barrier Reef occurs in January and February.

Heading south, the next climate area of the continent is sub-tropical, and then the seasons become more defined and temperate, with Tasmania, the southernmost tip of the continent, being the coolest. Summer in central Australia is unbearably hot, while the clear warm days of winter are the best time to visit.

DECIDING WHERE TO LIVE

Over ten million people live in the main cities of Melbourne, Sydney, Brisbane, Perth and Adelaide. Each city and large town has a wide choice of housing options and community services catering for every need. This guarantees that you and your family will find a suitable and very comfortable environment in which to live.

Design of houses

No matter how demanding your requirements, the high standard and wide choice of properties to rent or purchase and the relatively low housing prices will satisfy most requirements. Even a relatively modest house in Australia will have a swimming pool and plenty of garden area. The surrounding community area will usually have playing fields and tennis courts available for the use of the locals. The houses typically combine European and American style with an Australian twist. Building materials and designs for houses vary throughout the country in relation to the climate. In Queensland's tropical climate, the houses tend to be open plan and constructed of timber. In Melbourne, where the weather may encapsulate four seasons in one day, many homes have fireplaces and are built of brick. Garaging or undercover parking is important, especially near the coast where the salt air will rust vehicles. Historical houses built of wood or sandstone, dating from the early nineteenth century, are known as 'Federation' and, because they are well regarded, will cost more than a 1960s-style bungalow.

Because the traditional goal of a 'home on a quarter-acre block of land' has strongly influenced the format of the suburbs in most of Australia's towns and cities, there is a great sense of space and privacy. Therefore the communities within cities are very comfortable places to reside.

Until recently, the inner-city areas throughout Australia were used purely for commercial or business reasons. Only in the last 20 years have people discovered the excitement and convenience of inner-city living, therefore high-rise apartment blocks are not as common as in Asia, America and Europe and are usually more upmarket.

As in other large cosmopolitan cities in the world, housing is more expensive in the centre of the city than in the smaller towns; for example, property in Melbourne or Sydney would cost more than double that in the city of Hobart.

The advantage of living in a large city like Sydney is the wide choice of property available, from waterside mansions and suburban homes to convenient and comfortable inner-city apartments. The best way to evaluate the housing market is to contact your local Australian Mission for the latest information. This means that you will be able to find the house of choice in the best area for you and your family, offering the lifestyle you want, at a suitable price.

A recent poll conducted by UMR Research found that nearly 60% of Australians want immigration programmes that encourage settlement in areas outside of Melbourne and Sydney. Because of environmental pressures, rising house prices, failings in power and water supplies, Sydney residents would like Australia to give priority to new immigrants who are prepared to settle in areas such as Darwin and Tasmania.

The Northern Territory

The Northern Territory offers a lot – healthy lifestyle, modern infrastructure, a youthful and multicultural population and a dynamic economy. With twice as much land area as France but a population of only 210,674, the Territory consists of a huge wilderness dotted with outposts of civilisation – mines, Aboriginal settlements, cattle stations, and great national parks. The capital, established in 1869, is Darwin. Visitors travel through this region to visit Alice Springs, Uluru Rock (Ayers Rock) and the Kakadu National Park. The area enjoys a very tropical climate but, like most tropical destinations, has been affected by the natural elements, the most infamous being cyclone Tracey in 1974.

The Northern Territory's significant industry sectors include tourism, mining, construction, agriculture, pastoral and horticulture. This Territory acts as the closest capital city to link with major Asian centres because of its geographical location, and is forging ahead with business connections as a result.

South Australia

South Australia, the first Australian State to be founded by the free settlers, is a region famous for vineyards (Barossa Valley), producing award-winning wines and brandy. An exceptional lifestyle and a modern economy is found in this State. The very attractive capital Adelaide (population 1,568,204) was designed and created in 1836 by British Army engineer, Colonel William Light. Most of South Australia's population lives in or near to Adelaide, so travelling outside the city environs gives the experience of the real outback. Adelaide has an extraordinary range of performance venues and is world renowned for the Womad, (music) Fringe, and wine festivals. The capital's world-class education and research facilities, coupled with the innovative technology of the region, offer a competitive, productive and creative location for business migrants. The South Australian Government is working with potential investors to identify growth markets and possible partners, and is committed to fast-track approval for new projects and businesses by providing financial incentives and tailored support.

Australian Capital Territory

Australian Capital Territory was purpose built in 1911 as the country's national capital on the southern coast where some of Australia's most attractive beaches can be found. The national capital was strategically placed in the south-east region between the busy markets of Melbourne and Sydney in preparation for future major growth and expansion. The capital, Canberra, heart of the Australian Government, administration and international affairs, is an important business centre. Taking decades to complete, this is a totally planned city, originally designed by Chicago architect Walter Burley Griffin. Canberra (the Aboriginal translation means woman's breasts), includes politicians, diplomats, public servants and academics amongst its growing population of 334,225, of which 40% are under 26 years of age. Home to a number of institutes, including the National Library, the National Gallery, the Australian War Memorial, the High Court and the Federal Parliament, Canberra, because of lengthy and careful planning, combines modern city living and a cosmopolitan lifestyle with a safe community in a clean environment.

Queensland

Queensland, or the Sunshine State, stretches from the tropical rain forests in the north, through the deserts to the Pacific coastline and to the northeast and the border that is the Great Barrier Reef. This State is renowned for the extremes of cosmopolitan city living on the one hand and the slower pace of life in small towns and settlements on the other. Queensland's total population is 4,091,546. Over one and a half million people live in the capital Brisbane, which has grown from penal beginnings to being Australia's third largest city today. People are attracted to this city because of the quality of life, which includes beaches, islands, beautiful weather, fresh yet cheap food, easy-to-use transport and many business opportunities. As Australia's fastest growing State, the economic activity and growth is in tourism, manufacturing, technology, primary industry and services.

Victoria

Victoria, the smallest of the mainland States, has a population of 5,128,310. Three million people reside in the capital, Melbourne, which was established in 1835 and is now Australia's second largest city, a gracious and refined 'European'-like centre of finance, fashion, food and theatre. The colony of Victoria was originally settled by gold miners around the Ballarat and Bendigo regions, farmers and herders in the Murray and Goulburn Valleys, and mainly whalers and sealers at Apollo Bay and Port Fairy. Located at the bottom of Australia on the coast, Melbourne's climate is a mixture of temperature extremes sometimes experiencing each of the four seasons in one day. The city is a very popular and attractive place to live with gardens, culture, beautiful architecture, arts, fashion and a growing business economy.

Western Australia

Western Australia, about the size of Western Europe, is a huge and empty State, whose primary wealth derives from large mining and mineral concerns, with flourishing manufacturing, tourism and primary industries. Almost three-quarters of the total population of over two and a half million live in the capital Perth. Geographically the most remote city in the world, Perth is separated from the rest of Australia by the barren expanse of the Nullarbor Plains. Migrants moving to Perth enjoy a near perfect climate with clean air, low living costs, and a superb

Mediterranean-type lifestyle. The beautiful beaches and rivers are close to the city, so it is easy to escape from the hurly burly of the business world.

New South Wales

New South Wales, Australia's most populous State, with a population of nearly seven million people, offers contrasts of snow on the Southern Alps, dust storms in the west and monsoons in the northeast. Hunters Valley, the wine growing area, is renowned for the fine full-bodied reds and dry whites like Semillon.

Bathurst, Australia's oldest inland town, was founded in 1815 and now hosts the world-renowned annual car-racing event. Australia's unique service 'The Flying Doctor' originated in Broken Hill, where the world's largest silver, lead and zinc lodes are mined.

Sydney's dry summer temperatures can reach 30 degrees centigrade (90 degrees F) and in winter fall to 12 degrees C (50 degrees F), with snow on the southern ranges. Famous for the spectacular Opera House and Harbour Bridge, the longest and widest single-span bridge in the world, which joins Sydney's northern and southern suburbs, this bustling, exciting city of nearly four million is one of the world's biggest by land mass. Living magnificently by world standards, 'Sydneysiders' enjoy a full social and cultural calendar. The annual Gay Mardi Gras attracts over 600,000 people to watch floats of fabulously attired transvestites and other gay folk, such as the Dikes on Bikes, strut their stuff.

National parks and a spectacular 60-kilometre coastline surround this spacious city. The populace chooses to either live in areas ranging from the harbour to the beaches and further out suburbs, or the quieter, more relaxed suburban lifestyles. Because Sydney has Australia's most influential central business district, many national and international offices are located here. Regarded as an international gateway, millions of tourists arrive at Sydney's airport to begin their Australian travel experience. Beautiful Sydney offers the benefits of a large city: fun, excitement, hustle, and lots of culture coloured with the locals' renowned laid-back attitude.

In September 2000, the world focused on Sydney as host of the spectacular XXVII Olympiad Games, one of the most celebrated to date. The Games were a tremendous success for Australia as 3.5 billion people worldwide watched via television networks. The total economic benefit to Australia was estimated at over six billion dollars and with over 15,000 media representatives covering the event, the Games showed Sydney to be a first-class modern city of the world.

Tasmania

Tasmania (population 489,922), an island 300km off the south-eastern tip of Australia and separated from the continent by the Bass Strait, is a beautiful, temperate, green island. Unspoilt and unpolluted, Tasmania has the cleanest air and water of the inhabited world. The island has an enormous amount of forests, mountains and fertile farmlands that are protected as reserves and National Parks. Hobart, (population 203,600), Tasmania's capital and Australia's second oldest city after Sydney, is located at the most southern part of the island and has become famous in recent years for the New Year's Day annual Sydney to Hobart Yacht Race. Before 1840, Scottish settlers had built the oldest golf course in the Southern Hemisphere and today there are over 80 spectacular courses set amongst the rain forests, rural landscapes, close to deserted beaches or near the mountains. Tasmania produces some of the world's finest wool and food products, and sells advanced technology and products to more than 40 international niche markets.

The official tourist organisation in each of the above states or territories will provide information on climate, festivals and upcoming events. For more information on services available in your neighbourhood, contact your local library, or council. Or visit the website: *www.nla.gov.au/ oz/gov/local.html*

BUYING OR RENTING?

Once you have decided where (which State or Territory) you want to live in Australia, renting for 6–12 months is usually the best option while you decide which locality you want to live in. Some immigrants visit Australia before the final move and gain local knowledge through a friendly real estate agent and/or utilise the Internet. Others stay with family or friends already settled in Australia or may opt to stay in a motel until they decide where they will live.

Most real estate agents have a rental section within their offices that deals solely with houses, units and apartments.

Apartments are often called 'units'. It is fairly easy to locate a suitable property from the available and extensive range. Other places to research and find rental houses are the local and national daily newspapers, where advertisements for 'To Let' and 'Accommodation Vacant' usually appear on Wednesdays and Saturdays. Also check community notice boards and the Internet. See *www. home.priceguide.com.au, www.workingin-australia.com, www.lg.tafensw.edu.au, www.craigslist.org*

The lease

When you have found your new home (whether it be rented or purchased) you and your family will settle and feel more secure. For a rental property, a lease will have to be signed and you may be required to pay a bond of four weeks' rent. The bond is refundable when you leave the premises, as long as there is no damage and the property is clean. Rent is usually paid two to four weeks in advance. *The lease is legally binding so make sure you understand the terms and conditions before you sign it. If in doubt seek professional advice.* Some States have a tenancy advocate service for advice on your obligations and rights.

Home ownership

Home ownership is the norm in Australia, with over 70% of the population in many cities owning their property. If you decide to buy, banks, credit unions, building societies and other financial institutions offer up to 90% of the value of the property, depending on the borrower's financial status. (See Chapter 17.)

Estate agents

Real estate agents, who are licensed and governed by

regulations sell most houses and units in Australia. It is worth noting the following points:

- They work both for the buyer and seller and will introduce buyers to owners who want to sell their property.

- They find property for buyers, arrange inspections, conduct negotiations, and usually determine all matters relevant to the transaction (e.g. title search, legality of structure), present a written offer, negotiate to obtain the lowest possible price for the property, prepare and explain the Contract for the Sale of Land, liaise with all parties, including solicitors, to facilitate settlement, explain any time extensions for finance approval or settlement and monitor the contract from sale to settlement.

- They manage property for lease or rental.

- Real estate contracts or selling agent agreements *are worded to protect the rights and obligations* of the seller and the agent.

- The agreement will detail the name of the vendor/owner, the property details, the agreed fee for the agent on finding a purchaser, terms and conditions detailing the rights and obligations of the agent and the vendor and any agreement relating to the marketing costs which the seller pays.

- Fees are not set by the Government but are between the agent and the principal of the company who holds the Real Estate Agent License.

- The fee is dependent on the quality and quantity of services appropriate to the property for sale.

- The vendor/seller pays the agent's fee.

- Look for services that you feel comfortable with to help you find a property over a reasonable time period, at a reasonable cost and for a fair fee.

- Do your homework and research as much as you can by talking to others who have already purchased.

This is only an outline of what to expect when purchasing property in Australia. It is advisable to speak to experts and find out as much as possible before buying, but be assured it is a reasonably straightforward process and you will find that your money will go a lot further than in the UK.

Some States have professional buyer's agents who will locate and negotiate the purchase of a new property for a fee. Often former valuers or real estate agents, they are generally knowledgeable, but may be expensive. Fees vary, but the full service generally requires a registration fee and a percentage of the purchase price. For example, a house valued from A$501,000 to A$750,000 would have an initial fee of A$2,200 up front, then 1.7% of the purchase price. If the agent is successful in buying you a house at auction, a payment of A$22,750 and a percentage of the total purchase will make up the fee. However, in the long run, this service may save you time and money, and reduce stress.

Buying a house

Buying a house is a major commitment, so you need to be familiar with the area you want to live, schools and universities and transport, but again you will usually have plenty of choice and get excellent value for your money. Properties for sale are listed with real estate agencies or in the newspapers.

Purchasing property in Australia is usually a simple and straightforward process that can be speedily completed. Usually a solicitor or conveyancer is usually required to check the title deeds and organise the paperwork. *Again do not sign anything until you are fully aware of the terms and conditions of the contract.* English people may assume that making an offer to purchase a house is the same as in the UK where the initial contract is not really binding. *An Offer to Purchase is a legal and binding contract.* If the offer is accepted you are obliged to purchase the house. Another option is to purchase by auction which, according to various current television programmes in different states, appears to be very popular. Remember that the valuation, legal and conveyancing fees will need to be paid for. The agent's fee and stamp duty, which is applicable in some States, are usually paid for by the vendor.

For further advice on purchasing a home The Home Purchase Advisory Service (tel: 1800 806 653; free call in Australia) provides free information, as do a range of free publications such as *The A–Z of Home Purchase*, and *Financing Your Home Purchase*.
Home Buyers' Checklist: *www.firstnet.info/freeguides/*,

www.archicentre.co.au, www.housing.nsw.gov.au/Home+ Buying + and + Building, email: *advisory@housing.nsw.gov.au*

Building your own house

The Federal Government encourages residents to build their own home. Home loan finance is available to fund the purchase of land and construction of a dwelling through the major banks – Commonwealth, Westpac, ANZ and National Bank. The smaller community-based banks often offer very competitive rates and a more personalised service. Other companies such as Advantage Credit Union, Aussie Home Loans, AXA Home Loans, Suncorp-Metway and Wizard Home Loans also offer comparable rates and loans. Be aware that *rates first quoted by a lending institution may change before you actually sign* the loan paperwork. And compare establishment fees and monthly service fees from each institution, as these are extremely variable. A 'Construction Loan' will fund the different stages of building the house. Make sure you use only licensed contractors for all building and related work, e.g. architect, plumber and builder.

Home village displays

A popular method of purchase or of building your home is to visit a Home Village Display. Sydney boasts the world's largest home and display villages, with up to one hundred designs on show, so you can easily find your dream home. The exhibition houses on display in the villages are examples of the skills of Australia's biggest, most respected and specialist builders and showcase the latest designs and best-selling homes.

The advantage of this type of display is that you can choose the design you like and the best type of building materials for the area you have chosen to live in, and view the home as it will be when completed. This 'one stop' shop enables you to choose a block of land from dozens of locations, and arrange finance on the spot. To visit the two major display villages in Sydney you can contact the manager of HomeWorld and at *www.homeworld.com.au*

Home World
Kellyville
NWS 2155
Tel: 006129629 4822

If you are building outside of Sydney, then a visit to these exhibition homes is recommended as many builders construct homes all over New South Wales. For up-to-date information on display villages both in and outside of Sydney, contact your local Australia mission.

Property prices
Property price growth is mixed across the capital cities. The growing demand for residential property is expected to fuel modest price growth for the next three years. The boom centres, Darwin and Perth, have weakening property markets, while growth is increasing in Queensland, with modest gains expected for Melbourne, Adelaide and Canberra.

BIS Shrapnel and Wizard Home Loans predicted that most major east-coast cities would experience price growth until 2010. The Sydney market is likely to be impacted by the existing high cost of housing, making properties beyond the reach of many buyers. However, higher interest rates and rate increases may affect growth overall.

For comparison of rates check out: *www.wizard.com.au*

The State of Victoria has introduced regulations which will require all new homes to have solar hot water heating, rainwater tanks and double-glazing or insulation to reduce energy consumption. These were implemented in July 2005.

Services you will need are electricity, gas, water, garbage and telephone. It is advisable to give as much notice as possible to the supplier, both for connection and cancelling. Some services may require a bond before you sign their contract.

16

Healthcare

PUBLIC HEALTH CARE SYSTEM

Established in 1984, Medicare provides Australians with one of the world's most comprehensive and highest quality health-care systems. Through Medicare, Australians have the benefit of free public hospital treatment and free or subsidised medical care that is available to everyone regardless of income, age, or health status. Medicare provides both free hospital and medical cover for permanent residents who are financially disadvantaged such as low-income earners and those receiving sickness or unemployment benefits, or age and invalid pensions. To help fund the scheme, resident taxpayers are subject to a Medicare Levy.

Treatment and admission to a public hospital is guaranteed for emergencies such as accidents, heart attacks or urgent surgery. Minor or less acute illnesses can also be treated within the public hospital system. Because of high demand for treatments on the public service, there are long waiting lists for elective surgery, so individuals cannot specify a time or date convenient to them for treatment.

Medicare
To enrol in Medicare you will need to take your passport and travel documents to your nearest Medicare office (*www.medicareaustralia.gov.au*). The address is listed in the phonebook and this needs to be done seven days after your arrival. If you are eligible, you will be given your Medicare number entitling you to free public hospital care and subsidised medicines and your card will arrive by mail in three weeks' time. Also ask for the available *Welcome Kit* which will explain Medicare, the requirements for benefits and payments and other government health services in 12 languages. Medicare does not cover ambulance costs, dental services, physiotherapy, spectacles, podiatry, chiropractic services or private hospital accommodation.

The Government offers a 30% rebate on private health insurance premiums and a 1% levy on high-income earners who do not have private health insurance, to encourage citizens to take financial responsibility for their health and reduce the burden on the tax system.

Lifetime health cover is a system of lower premiums, which may change, applicable to those under 30 years who take out and maintain private health insurance cover for their lifetime.

PRIVATE HEALTH INSURANCE

Private health insurance is available to anyone wanting to cover the costs of becoming a private patient.

Benefits are:

◆ Choice of your treating doctor.
◆ A reduced waiting time for elective surgery.
◆ Option of private hospital for treatment.
◆ Cover is provided for dental, optical, pharmaceutical, physiotherapy and a wide range of other services not covered by Medicare.

Approximately 34% of Australia's population choose private health care and of these 24% have cover with Medicare Private. There are other insurance companies providing cover, but Medicare Private's benefit is that their hospital insurance covers 100% of hospital charges, including extras like telephone calls, television rental and newspapers.

The Commonwealth Government regulates private health funds and all follow the principle of community rating where everyone pays the same. The premiums charged by the various funds do not vary according to age, sex, state of health or the size of your family. Consequently, a family premium is double the single premium regardless of family size and a young healthy single person will pay the same as an elderly, unwell, single person, provided they have taken out a similar cover.

Rules regarding membership of private health funds vary between States, so it is recommended that you research the most suitable cover for your requirements in the location that you decide to settle in.

More information is available from the following websites:

www.health.gov.au/privatehealth and *www.phiac.gov.au*
www.medicareaustralia.gov.au

WHERE TO GO IF YOU ARE SICK

General Practitioners
General Practitioners (GPs) are where you should go if it is not an emergency. Contact names and details are to be found in the *Yellow Pages* under 'Medical Practitioners' or your nearest medical centre. If your doctor prescribes antibiotics or any other medication you will be given a prescription to take to the nearest chemist or pharmacy. Immunisation is not compulsory, but is recommended for all children. Some States or Territories require a record of immunisation when a child begins school. Speak to your family doctor for more information. If necessary, your doctor may refer you to a specialist or other medical person for further treatment. A specialist cannot be seen without a doctor's referral.

Although the visit to your GP or specialist is not free, a rebate through Medicare is available. This rebate is 85% of the Medical Benefits Schedule (MBS) fee. The MBS sets down fees for services determined by the Government to be fair to both patient and the doctor. Low-income earners and those receiving benefits will receive a 'Health Care Card'. Holders of this card do not pay anything for a visit to the doctor, as the GP will directly bill Medicare for the rebate.

The Commonwealth Government also subsidises most prescription medications brought at pharmacies through a scheme called 'The Pharmaceutical Benefits Scheme', which provides access to prescription medication at a reasonable cost. Health Care Card holders pay a low set fee per prescription.

If you are being admitted to a public hospital then you should have your Medicare card with you, even if you have private health insurance. As a public patient at a public hospital you will need to contribute to the in-hospital charges and pay for extras like television and phone services. Medicare covers 75% of the hospital and medical charges.

If you have private health insurance, your doctor will usually make the hospital booking, and you will be required to fill out forms regarding your medical history and personal details. You may require pre-admission blood tests and X-rays. When you leave hospital, even if you have full insurance cover you may be asked to pay the difference between the insurance cover and the fees and if you do not have health insurance you will be asked to pay the anticipated costs before you are admitted.

Doctors and dentists
Doctors and dentists are in every area and can be found

in the *Yellow Pages* of the phone book. You may wish to take out private health insurance to help pay for any dentistry you require.

Emergencies

If you require emergency treatment, the emergency phone numbers of the nearest casualty (emergency) department attached to major hospitals or medical centres are inside the front cover of the *White Pages* telephone directory. *If an ambulance is required in an extreme emergency, dial 000 and do not hang up.* The ambulance service is provided free only to those on a government pension or low income earners who have a Health Care Card. It is advisable to join a *private health insurance* fund to cover the cost, as it may be expensive.

17

Banking and Financial Planning

It is advisable to speak with your current banking consultant to ascertain what contacts they have with banks in Australia, before you immigrate. Alternatively, before you leave home for your new country you may be able to arrange – using any of the websites below – ATM, (automatic transmission, which is advanced secure banking technology requiring a pin number), credit cards and bank accounts. You will also be able to organise the transfer of funds and insurances through the banks. Always ask two to three different companies for quotes and advice. A possible benefit of conducting all of your financial transactions through the bank is that there are no fees up front, although the cost may be included elsewhere!

AUSTRALIAN BANKS AND WEBSITE CONTACTS

◆ **Reserve Bank of Australia**
Monetary policy statements, economic statistics, description of the payment system, information on banknotes, and other publications and research. *http://www.rba.gov.au/*

◆ **Commonwealth Bank of Australia**
Offers personal banking, business solutions, institutional banking, company information and shareholder centre. *http://www.commbank.com.au*

◆ **National Australia Bank**
The largest bank in Australia, offering personal, business, agribusiness, and online financial services. *http://www.nab.com.au/*

◆ **Westpac Banking Corporation**
Offers online share trading, news, banking, calculators, and products. *http://www.westpac.com.au*

◆ **ANZ – Australia and New Zealand Banking Group Limited**
Offers home, car, and business loans, as well as Internet banking, insurance, and deposits products. *http://www.anz.com.au/*

◆ **Macquarie Bank**
Provides banking services for corporations, institutions, government, personal banking, investment, and business packages.
http://www.macquarie.com.au/

◆ **St George Bank**
Regional Australian bank offers commercial, personal,

wealth management solutions and banking services.
http://www.stgeorge.com.au/

◆ **Woolworths Ezy Banking**
Offers products, credit card, reward, where to bank,
and contact information.
http://www.ezybanking.com.au/

◆ **HSBC Bank Australia Limited**
Offering market research, personal, commercial financial services, electronic banking, and funds management. *http://www.hsbc.com.au/*

◆ **BankWest**
Provides personal, agribusiness, and business banking
in Western Australia. *http://www.bankwest.com.au/*

◆ **Elders International**
Bankers for the farming and real estate industry in
Australia. *http://www.elders.com.au/*

◆ **Rabobank Australia**
Includes solution services, Internet banking, AG
information, news, and branches.
http://www.rabobank.com.au/

◆ **Bendigo Bank**
Offers rewards, loan calculators, online share trading
and wealth management. Community bank with its
headquarters in regional Australia.
http://www.bendigobank.com.au/

◆ **ING Direct**
Delivers savings and investment products directly to
the consumers. *http://www.ingdirect.com.au/*

- **Suncorp Metway**
  A national finance, insurance, and banking corporation. Formerly Suncorp, Metway, and QIDC.
  http://www.suncorp.com.au/

- **American Express Australia**
  Offers online access to its world-class card, financial, insurance, and travel services.
  http://www.americanexpress.com.au/

- **Bank SA**
  Offers a range of financial products, wealth management, branch locator, business packages, and company details. *http://www.banksa.com.au/*

- **Bank of Queensland**
  Provides private and commercial banking services, loans, interest rates, company profile, and products.
  http://www.boq.com.au/

- **Adelaide Bank**
  A retail bank providing a range of professional financial services, with its head office in South Australia. *http://www.adelaidebank.com.au/*

- **Perpetual Trustees Australia**
  Provides investments, corporate trust, financial services, and news. *http://www.perpetual.com.au*

- **Citibank Australia**
  Provides a range of personal banking services, credit cards, insurance, and investments in Australia.
  http://www.citibank.com.au/

- **Virgin Credit Card**
  Offers no annual fee credit card, online banking, company profile, and online application.
  http://www.virginmoney.com.au/

- **Credit Union Australia**
  Includes financial products, banking tools, contact details, and interest rates. *http://www.cua.com.au/*

- **Australian National Credit Union**
  Includes rates and fees, tips, online application, police and nurses' new members information, and loans.
  http://www.australiancu.com/

- **Bank One Australia**
  Full service commercial bank active in corporate finance, international trade, risk management, capital markets and cash management.
  http://www.bankone.com.au/

- **Savings and Loans Credit Union**
  Provides banking products, loans, insurance, financial planning, and business banking.
  http://www.savingsloans.com.au/

- **Heritage Building Society**
  Provides loans, investments, netbanking, share trading, online forms calculators, and financial services.
  http://www.heritageonline.com.au/

- **Illawarra Mutual Building Society**
  Financial institution with branches in New South Wales, and Queensland. *http://www.imb.com.au/*

- **Newcastle Permanent Building Society**
  Services include banking, savings accounts, insurance, and financial advice throughout Australia.
  http://www.newcastlepermanent.com.au/

- **Elders Rural Bank**
  Offers Internet banking, latest news, financial specialist locator, and deposits.
  http://www.eldersruralbank.com.au/

- **Australian Central Credit Union**
  Offers a comprehensive range of personal financial products and services including loans, savings and investments, insurance, credit cards and financial planning. *http://www.accu.com.au*

- **Advance Funds Management**
  Specialist funds management arm of the St George Group. Provides a wide range of retail and wholesale-managed investments, superannuation, and pension products. *http://www.advance.com.au/*

- **Home Building Society**
  Offers savings and transaction accounts, telephone banking, online calculators, interest rates, and news.
  http://www.homedirect.com.au/

- **Bank of New Zealand Australia**
  Provides a full range of banking services to Australian businesses and has been operating in Australia since 1872. *http://www.bnza.com.au*

- **Wide Bay Capricorn Building Society**
  Includes Internet banking, news, special offers, products and services. *http://www.widebaycap.com.au/*

- **AMP Banking**
  Offers business banking, home loans, credit cards, savings account, and contact details.
  http://www.ampbanking.com.au

- **Leasepac Financial Services**
  Provides financing to businesses across Australia.
  http://www.leasepac.com.au/

- **First Australian Building Society**
  Consists of Northern Building Society in North Queensland, and First Provincial Building Society in Southern Queensland.
  http://www.firstaustralian.com.au/

- **SG Australia**
  Provides investment, and commercial banking services in Australia and New Zealand.
  http://www.sgaustralia.com.au/

- **TMT Partners**
  An independent investment bank providing strategic and financial advice to participants in the telecommunications, media and technology sectors in Australia.
  http://www.tmtpartners.com.au/

- **Bass and Equitable**
  Provides personal, phone, loan calculator, and business banking to the Tasmanian community.
  http://www.b-e.com.au/

- **Loancorp**
  Arranges a variety of financial solutions for brokers, and mortgage originators.
  http://www.loancorp.com.au/

- ◆ **Royal Guardian Mortgage Corporation**
  Offers loan calculator, inquiry form, and contact details. *http://www.royalguardian.com.au/*

- ◆ **Trustar Mortgage**
  Huge range of loans from personal and commercial requirements, apply online, product rates, and downloads. *http://www.trustar.com.au/*

- ◆ **Randwick Credit Union**
  Offers a loan calculator, interest rates, car loans, fees, and charges. *http://www.rcu.com.au/*

Other institutions and bankers are Bank of Melbourne, *www.bankofmelbourne.com.au*, Commonwealth Bank, *www.commbank.com.au*, *www.wizard.com.au* trustbank *www.trustbank.com.au*

FINANCIAL PLANNING
Financial planning is essential for understanding the differences between your present country and your new home in pensions, property, mortgages, tax, closing balance and Australian arrival values of tax and financial planning. *Before you emigrate it is recommended that you contact finance specialists for advice on fluctuating exchange rates.* Once you have decided on the move it is advisable to fix an exchange rate on a forward contract. Over quiet or holiday periods financial markets may become volatile and automated limit or stop loss orders can protect your funds. For more information contact: email: *www.hifx.co.uk*

Make sure that you also take advice on your pension plan, as a licensed pension transfer specialist will maximise your pension balance taking the exchange rate into consideration. Also check your insurances, especially life and endowment policies as they may not have to be surrendered/sold before you leave. Also your family will need insurance cover in transit. Overall tax planning including Capital Gains Tax needs to be advised on before leaving as well as on arrival. For more information contact your bank or financial adviser.

It may be advisable to contact different sources like the Commonwealth Bank of Australia: *www.commbank.com. au*, *www.miplo.co.uk* or email *londonmbs@cba. com.au* or *info@miplc.co.uk*

Loans

All lending institutions are required by law to provide full information on all interest charges and fees for the life of a loan. A comparison interest rate for all borrowings; car, home mortgage or personal loans must be provided so that consumers can evaluate the total long-term costs.

Getting good financial advice

Make sure that you only:

- ◆ Deal with a licensed advisory business, preferably one that is recommended by someone or by a business that you can trust.

- ◆ Pick the adviser with the strongest qualifications, experience and integrity.

- ◆ Ask questions until you totally understand the small print and the implications of the plan.

- If you feel uneasy, it's OK to walk away.

- Make sure your financial plan suits your needs and personality.

- When you get a good plan, stick to it.

- Keep all your paperwork.

INSURANCES

Insurance is strongly recommended to cover your house, the contents and your car. The law requires every car owner to have third party insurance as the absolute minimum. Also dental, health and sickness insurance is advisable. As it is against the law to sell the above services without a licence, make sure you deal only with a business that is licensed by the Government. If you have a complaint about any person or business who you feel has acted in an unscrupulous manner, contact the Australian Securities and Investments Commission (ASIC).

Taking out insurances

Checklist for choosing an insurance policy:

- Shop around to find the policy that best suits your needs for your
  – home
  – car
  – income.

- Make sure, if you're dealing with an insurer, broker or agent, that they hold an Australian Financial Services (AFS) licence or are an employee or authorised representative of an AFS licence holder.

- Make sure you are provided with a:
  - product disclosure statement
  - financial services guide
  - statement of advice.

- Make sure the insurer or insurance agent or broker has clearly explained the policy to you.

- Make sure you understand what the policy covers and what it doesn't.

- Find out whether the cost is competitive.

Choosing a credit card

Contact your bank for details. A credit card (or higher credit limit) is easy to obtain, or if you're after convenience but don't want debt, use a debit card instead. If you decide you want a credit card, you have the choice of two types: those with interest-free days and those which have no interest-free days.

Card type interest fees

- 'Interest free days'. Higher interest is charged either from the day you purchase or from the statement date unless you repay in full within the interest free period. Interest on cash advances is applied immediately. Generally higher fees apply.

- No 'interest free' days. Lower interest is charged from the date of purchase. Generally lower fees apply.

Cards with an interest-free period work best if you pay off your balance in full each month and avoid cash advances. The no-interest-free-period card will suit people who do not pay off their outstanding balances each month.

When is interest charged?

Interest is generally charged either from the date of purchase of items or from the date your monthly statement is issued. For cash advances, interest is usually charged from the date of the withdrawal. Insist on seeing a copy of the Conditions of Use before you apply, so you can check because, possibly, you will be better off with a card that only applies interest from the statement date.

Credit card fees

Watch out for fees (which must be properly disclosed.) Depending on how you use your card, fees can add a lot to the cost of your card. Commonly charged fees include:

◆ annual account fees
◆ fees to use rewards programmes
◆ fees for late payments
◆ payment dishonour fees
◆ fees for exceeding your credit limit.

Australian Securities and Investments Commission (FIDO)

The Financial Planning Association in Australia and a very useful site for investors: *www.fido.asic.gov.au* For a free copy of the booklet 'Getting Advice', email *infoline@asic.gov.au* with full name and address, phone 1300 300 630 or download the PDF.

TAX

Income tax rates for individuals

In Australia, a taxpayer's income is taxed progressively which means that higher-income earners pay more tax than lower-income earners. This is achieved by taxing a range of income brackets (tax brackets) at a set percentage or cents in the dollar. The rate of tax within these brackets is called the marginal rate of tax. For Australian residents, the first tax bracket, from A$0 to A$6,000, has a zero marginal rate of tax. Tax is applied to every dollar after this figure. This tax-free amount is called the tax-free threshold.

Residents
These rates apply to individuals who:

♦ are residents of Australia for tax purposes for the whole financial year, and

♦ did not leave full-time education for the first time during the financial year.

Taxable income rates 2007–08

A$0 – A$6,000	Nil
A$6,001 – A$30,000	15c for each A$1 over A$6,000
A$30,001 – A$75,000	A$3,600 plus 30c for each A$1 over A$30,000
A$75,001 – A$150,000	A$17,100 plus 40c for each A$1 over A$75,000
A$150,001 and over	A$47,100 plus 45c for each A$1 over A$150,000

For more information go to *www.ato.gov.au*

The above rates do not include the Medicare levy of 1.5%.

Superannuation
Since July 2007 Australians are able to benefit from the

changes to superannuation (the 'Better Super') to improve their retirement lifestyle. The reforms simplify the rules and give each individual more flexibility and choice in managing their savings. For more information go to *www.ato.gov.au/bettersuper/*

CONSUMER RIGHTS

Consumer rights are covered by law and action can be taken by the ombudsman offices to prevent unjust, unlawful or discriminatory treatment. The Human Rights and Equal Opportunity Commission (HREOC, *www.hreoc.com.au*) administers commonwealth law covering privacy, human rights, anti-discrimination, and social justice. The Australian Competition and Consumer Commission (ACCC, *www.accc.gov.au*) protects consumers to a certain degree against unsafe product, unfair and anti-competitive pricing and market practices.

Contact numbers within Australia for the following may be obtained by phoning Directory Enquiries

Commonwealth Ombudsman
Human Rights & Equal Opportunity Commission
Australian Banking Industry Ombudsman
Banking Insurance and Investment Assistance
Credit Union Dispute Resolution Centre
Credit Union Dispute Resolution Ombudsman
Insurance Enquiries and Complaints
Superannuation Complaints Tribunal (SCT)
Department of Fair Trading
Australian Competition & Consumer Commission

The Commonwealth Information Directory is a useful source of information about services for rural Australia.

18

Moving to Australia

SHIPPING

International moving is very different from the ordinary domestic move. Specialist companies whose main business is overseas removal are often able to offer competitive rates as they frequently ship consignments to other countries. These companies generally have depots throughout the UK and will be able to provide a free estimate of the costs involved. They provide experienced packers, containers and use export-quality heavy-duty materials for wrapping.

◆ Ensure the firm you choose is a member of the Overseas Group of the British Association of Removers (BAR, *www.bar.co.uk*), or the Federation of International Moving (FIDI). For more information go to *www.1-directory-international-movers.com*

- Make sure the company has suitable insurance such as the International Movers Mutual Insurance (IMMI). It is important to ensure that insurance cover commences once payment has been made, so that there are no extra costs when you receive the shipment in your new country.

- If time and speed are important, goods can be sent by airfreight, which will be expensive.

- Costs can be reduced if the company you choose offers a groupage container service, where the space is shared by other shipments going to the same destination.

- Check that you have marine insurance cover in the event of an unforeseen accident in transit or other problems such as delays.

- To save you time, money and unnecessary red tape ask your moving company to arrange Customs clearance, and transit bonds (required to ensure transit through foreign ports).

- Some companies will arrange for a destination agent to take care of your property and complete all the paperwork for delivery to your new address.

Start thinking and planning the removal at least three to six months before your departure by contacting different companies for information packs. Approach two or three firms for an estimate and remember it may take two to three weeks for the appointment date. It is important that you have an initial idea of the items you want shipped, although the estimator will guide you.

DECIDING WHAT TO TAKE

What to take is a major decision as it is expensive to ship goods that will prove unnecessary in your new country. It is important to have some familiar items to help your family settle. Ask friends in Australia for suggestions and remember that quality furniture and some household items will be more expensive to purchase in your new country. You may decide to take household goods like furniture, linen, crockery, cutlery and furnishings (rugs, curtains), your car (see below) and children's favourite toys. The moving company Allied Pickfords sell a children's storybook called *Moving Overseas* which will help small children to understand the move.

Quarantine regulations prohibit the import of products made of animal or plant matter, or religious/cultural artefacts. Large amounts of coins/money will need to be declared. Your shipping agent will be able to advise you on all of the above.

Electrical appliances

Electrical appliances function in Australia on the same 220/250 volts AC50HZ cycles as the UK, but the plug will need to be changed. If you plan to take electrical equipment like a CD player, hairdryer or television make sure that the items are compatible with Australia's electrical system. Video recorders need to be converted to receive Australian TV broadcasts and the television receiver needs to be converted to Australian frequency. Phones of all sorts are difficult and one of the biggest problems with any of the above is the extremes of temperature shipments encounter on the long voyage to Australia. New mobile services and the extensive networks in Australia ensure that you will have access to the latest technology in your new home.

Deciding whether to take your car

An important decision is whether to take your car or start anew. Would you be able to obtain spare parts in Australia and have it serviced satisfactorily? Find out if it is suitable to export from the contact details below or your shipping company. The car must have been owned and driven in the UK for 12 months or more. For permanent residency there is a one-car-per-person criteria. Import approval is required and this will take approximately four weeks. Shipping and insurance costs are payable in the UK. In Australia approximately 15% duty is payable on the UK purchase price and 10% GST may be payable on the UK purchase price, duty and shipping costs. Also payable are other costs which include port clearance, unpacking, quarantine inspection, MOT/roadworthy certification and registration.

Contact reputable freight companies for written quotes. They will arrange the export once you have the Department of Transport and Regional Services (DOTRS) approval. A car is safest shipped in a sealed 20-foot container, and any contents you want to pack inside travel free of charge. Usually the car will have mats, seat covers and bags of silica desiccant as protection against condensation damage. Motorbikes are normally shipped in wooden crates and again personal items can be packed inside. Costs payable in the UK include moving your car from your home to the warehouse where it will be packed into a container, and shipping and marine insurance cover (normally between 1–2% of the car's value). Costs in

Australia include unpacking the container, port charges, Customs clearance and quarantine procedures. Transit will take three to four weeks from the UK to Australia. Local Australian Customs brokers can assist you, and your shipping company may have suitable contacts to simplify the procedure.

TAKING YOUR PETS

Pets don't have to be left behind and moving them is fairly straightforward. More than a million of our furry and feathered friends safely fly worldwide each year. It is important to allow plenty of time, more than six months, for reservations to be made and all documentation to be completed. A reputable company will have a vet in attendance, provide boarding and grooming if required, use International Air Transport Association (IATA) approved travel kennels and offer collection of your animal. Again ask different companies for advice and costs.

For further information contact the official website *www.defra.gov.uk* and *www.parair.co.uk*, *http://www.airpets.com*, *www.ladyhaye.co.uk*. Email: *parair@btinternet.com*, *Airpets@compuserve.com*, *info@ladyhaye.co.uk* For import/export quarantine standards see *www.animalairlines.co.uk*, *www.csiro.com*

DEPARTURE AND ARRIVAL CHECKLISTS

Departure
- ◆ Check that all of your financial, taxation and legal matters are finalised. Check insurances.

- If travelling/arriving on a holiday check what facilities/services are available.

- Back up all important information on laptop/computer.

- Make sure all your travel plans are complete. Give your new contact details to your family and friends before you leave.

- Ensure you have all your original documents like birth certificates, university or similar degrees and awards, trade qualifications, family medical records, references and children's school reports. Make copies of all of your documents to keep in a safe place.

Arrival

Things to do as soon as possible after arrival in your new country:

- Apply for a Tax File Number – website *www.ato.gov. au/individuals* or phone the Australian Taxation Office (ATO) 13 28 61 for an application form to be posted to you.

- Register with Medicare and/or private health insurance see Chapter 14).

- Open a bank account if you haven't already done so.

- Enrol your children in school.

- Apply for a driver's licence.

Arriving in Australia

Nearly all visitors to Australia arrive by air; the main international airports are: Adelaide, Brisbane, Cairns, Darwin, Hobart, Melbourne, Perth and Sydney.

On board your aircraft you will be handed an arrival card called an 'Incoming Passenger Card'. Every person entering the country must fill out one of these. At each airport there are services to help you with information, car rental, hotel bookings, internal flights, taxis and bus services into the city. Passports that are current are required by all visitors, as are onward or return tickets and enough money to support them during their entire visit.

VISAS

All visitors to Australia require visas; the only exception is a New Zealand passport holder who is allowed entry with just a passport. Visitor visas are valid for visits of up to three months. If you are travelling for longer you will require a visa for a maximum period of six months. Rates will vary depending on your nationality.

Tourist visas are issued by the Australian Consulate/High Commission Office within your country and must be obtained before you leave home. If you think you might stay more than three months, it's best to get the longer visa before departure, because once you get to Australia, visa extensions will cost extra. You may also be asked to prove you have adequate funds to support yourself. If you're visiting immediate family who live in Australia apply for a Close Family Visa, which has fewer restrictions. If you need to extend your visa, contact DIMIA, the Department of Immigration and Multicultural and Indigenous Affairs.

Inoculations

Inoculations are generally not required unless during the two weeks before your arrival you have been in a country infected with typhoid, yellow fever, smallpox or cholera.

CUSTOMS REGULATIONS

At the time you receive your arrival card you will also be given a 'Travellers Statement'. This must be read, filled out and carefully adhered to. Each traveller may bring in the following articles free of tax and duty, providing that they are not intended for commercial purposes and that they accompany you through Customs:

- ◆ 1 litre of alcohol liquor – beer, wine or spirits – per person over 18 years of age.

- All personal clothes and footwear – excluding fur apparel.

- Articles for personal grooming and hygiene – excluding perfume concentrate and jewellery.

- All visitors' goods provided you intend to take them out of the country when you leave.

- Articles taken out of Australia on departure but not including articles purchased duty and/or sales tax free in Australia – any duty/tax free goods are counted against your duty free allowance.

- Other articles (not tobacco or alcohol) obtained overseas or duty and sales free in Australia up to and not exceeding a total purchase price of A$400 per person 18 years or older, or A$200 per person under 18 years. Please note this does include goods intended as gifts or received as gifts, and jewellery, whether personal, a gift or carried on behalf of others.

Members of the same family travelling together can complete one statement, that is a husband, wife and children under 18 years of age. They may also combine their individual duty free allowances.

Travellers may bring in more than their allocated amount, including tobacco and alcohol, as long as they declare the excess and pay the duty and/or tax owing. Unaccompanied baggage whether posted or shipped does not attract any duty free concessions unless you have owned and have used the items for 12 months or more.

Australia has strict laws prohibiting and restricting the entry of drugs, steroids, firearms and other weapons. If you are carrying goods that you think may fall into any of these categories or are subject to quarantine, then you must declare this to Customs upon your arrival.

There are no restrictions to the amount of currency that can be taken in or out of Australia; however, amounts of A$5,000 or more must be reported on arrival or departure.

Agricultural restrictions

Agricultural restrictions, enforced by the Quarantine Department, strive to maintain the pest, plant and animal disease-free status of most South Pacific countries. Australia has strict quarantine laws that apply to fruit, vegetables, fresh and packaged food, seed and some animal products. It is safest to assume that anything of a plant or animal nature is prohibited. If unsure check with Customs. Expect to be welcomed into the country with the ritual on-board pesticide spray.

Departure Tax

Departure Tax is paid by all travellers, either in your airline ticket cost or at the airport before you leave. Currently the departure tax stands at A$25.

(20)

Lifestyle

Lifestyle is what living in Australia is about. Most Australians live near the coast and regard leisure as crucial to their way of life. The relaxed weekends consisting of blue skies, wonderful beaches (Sydney has 70 easily accessible beaches), sea breezes, super cafés and restaurants, the ubiquitous barbecue and masses of fresh seafood contribute to the easy-going casual attitude of most Australians. With more urbanisation than anywhere else in the world, most Australians own their roomy homes, often with a swimming pool, on a large plot of land. The cities, where 80% of the population live, are very safe and clean compared with other similar-sized places in the world.

LEISURE ACTIVITIES

The arts

Australia has drawn its population from more than 120 countries from around the world, and its culture and arts reflect this vast resource. With government support, drama, film, music, literature and the visual arts have flourished and now reflect the collective national pride and voice of Australia's rich and diverse heritage. Museums all over the country focus on the maritime, technological, cultural and natural history. The capital cities boast an abundance of art galleries, repositories of fine Australian and international paintings and sculptures.

The Australian Ballet and Theatre Companies are renowned and regularly tour worldwide to other major cities and festivals. Joan Sutherland, Nicole Kidman, Russell Crowe, Kylie Minogue and Mel Gibson are famous Australians. The film industry is thriving with hits such as *Babe*, *Picnic at Hanging Rock* and *Moulin Rouge* and everyone is familiar with the Australian soaps.

Aussies are keen shoppers and all the fashion labels are available at the many large shopping malls and centres. Casinos and pubs are well patronised, as are the rugby league clubs. Every leisure and sporting activity known to man is available all year round in this ultimate playground environment.

Boating

The large expanse of water surrounding Australia, ideal weather, plentiful and secure anchorages and abundant inland waterway systems entice the majority of Australia's population to spend a lot of time around, in and on the water. Australia is renowned as a nation of 'boaties' and 'yachties' and boat ownership reflects this, with facilities for every class of boat from dinghies to multi-million-dollar yachts and cruisers. Registration is compulsory for all boats capable of ten knots or more, and drivers are required to hold a general boating licence and have a thorough knowledge of local rules and conditions. The Boating Industry Association is represented in most States and they offer advice and assistance in the purchase and ownership of all types of boats.

Golf

Australia has over one thousand courses around the country and many are world class, designed to test both the casual and more serious players. The ranges are often situated in beautiful locations. The Cypress Lakes and Country Club, located in the Hunter Valley 130kms north of Sydney, is a demanding course with the advantage of being situated in the heart of the Hunter Valley Wine District. This golf range, like many others, provides a pleasant backdrop to both social and business activities. Some courses are incorporated in resorts and accept casual players only, others are more established member-based clubs only and do not accept new members. Fortunately newer clubs with excellent fairways are actively pursuing new membership. Tasmania has over 80 golf courses.

Motoring

Australia is one of the most motorised countries in the world, because of the distances between work, home and social events. Much of the population takes advantage of the good quality roads and highways to tour the wide-open spaces of Australia. Motoring clubs abound and information on these is available at your local community council or information office.

Fishing

With the amount of water easily accessible on the coastline and inland waterways, fishing is the most popular leisure activity in Australia. Some of the best sea fishing does not require a boat as you can easily catch a wide range of fish from the beaches and rocks in your local area. Licences are required, also check the size limits and no-go areas. Penalties for breaking the law are severe. The ultimate fish is the black marlin, which can grow beyond 700kg and is renowned in the fishing world for being a great fighter. Trout fishing is generally restricted to the Snowy Mountain region in New South Wales, with popular brown, brook and rainbow trout found in these rivers. The Murray River cod is a freshwater fishermen's dream, where specimens as large as 1.8 metres long and weighing over 100kg been caught.

Horse racing

There is a great range of opportunities to be involved in racing, (part of the Australian psyche), from owning a thoroughbred horse, to having a punt at the local racecourse. The once a year, nation-stopping Melbourne Cup has become increasingly popular and now draws horses from as far away as Ireland. Held in November 'The Cup' has become a folk festival as much as a fiercely competitive horse race. Australians are amongst the greatest gamblers on Earth, with the turnover climbing to over A$7 billion a year at the Totaliser Agency Board (TAB). A percentage of this money is now being returned to race clubs as prize money or to improve facilities for both the race-going public and the horses.

Sports

Australia is a sporting nation. Not only do Australians play sport, but they watch sport, bet on sport and talk sport probably more than anything else. The climate, natural opportunities and adequate leisure time all provide the perfect framework for sporting activities. There are only a few countries in the world where you can take part in such a variety of sports and with such ease over the entire year. There is a large number of sporting clubs and teams available, from community-based projects, business social teams and club sports through to professionals, so if you enjoy sport then you will be able to find an activity that fits into your schedule.

Popular sports include soccer, rugby, Aussie rules, golf, tennis, bowls, basketball, netball and athletics. The mountains of New South Wales, Tasmania and Victoria offer horse treks in the summer and skiing in the winter. The beaches around Australia offer surfing, windsurfing, swimming and scuba diving, and the rivers and harbours are also places to sail and water-ski. Jogging and walking are national pastimes. All the major cities have beautiful gardens and there are great tracks and walkways through the mountainous and coastal areas as well.

$$\left(21 \right)$$

Useful Information

MONEY MATTERS

◆ Since 1966 Australia has had decimal currency –
dollars and cents. Coins are available in 5c, 10c, 20c,
50c, A$1 and A$2 pieces and notes come in A$5, A$10,
A$20, A$50 and A$100 denominations.

◆ Traveller's cheques and credit cards such as American
Express, MasterCard, Visa and Diners Club are
accepted. Most foreign currencies can be changed at
the airport, city banks, international class hotels and
Bureaux de Change, but make sure you have enough
money before travelling around Australia as these
services are usually only supplied in major tourist places.

◆ ATMs (automatic teller machines) are easily located for
cash and withdrawals can also be done using your Pin
(personal identification number) or bankcard. Your Pin
Number must be memorised or kept securely away from
your bankcard. Report any loss immediately.

- Shops usually open between 8 and 9a.m. and close between 5 and 6p.m. Monday – Friday. Shop hours are usually 9a.m. to 4p.m. on Saturday and Sunday. Late night shopping is usually Thursday or Friday until 9p.m. once a week.

- Business hours for government departments, post offices and offices are usually five days a week from 9a.m. –5p.m. Banks open 9a.m. – 4p.m. and 5p.m. on Fridays, with most businesses closed on public holidays. Small grocery stores and petrol stations that offer basic food and fuel are usually open longer hours, up to 24 hours a day, seven days a week.

- Postal service details for each area can be found in the front pages of the telephone directory.

- Tipping in Australia is at your discretion and generally only expected in taxis, restaurants and hotels. If you have had excellent service a tip is appropriate and most appreciated.

MEDIA

Since Australia is such an ethnically diverse society, newspapers, television and radio programmes are available in a number of different communities and languages.

Newspapers

There are two daily national newspapers:

The Australian. Website: *http://www.theaustralian.com.au/*
The Financial Review. Website: *http://www.afr.com.au/*

Each State and city has its own publication.

Sydney: *The Sydney Morning Herald.*
Website: *www.smh.com.au* and *Telegraph Mirror.*
Melbourne: *The Melbourne Age.* Website: *www.theage.com .*
au and *Herald Sun.* Website: *www.heraldsun.com.au*
Adelaide: *The Adelaide Advertiser.*
Website: *www.theadvertiser.news.com.au*
Brisbane: *The Brisbane Courier Mail.*
Website: *www.thecouriermail.news.com.au*
Perth: *The West Australian.*
Website: *www.thewestaustralian.com.au*
Hobart: *The Hobart Mercury.*
Website: *www.themercury.news.com.au*
Canberra: *The Canberra Times.*
Website: *http://www.canberratimes.com.au/*
Northern Territory: Northern Territory News.
Website: *www.ntnews.com.au*

Television

Depending on the location in Australia there are up to five television stations which include: three commercial channels, one ABC channel and one multicultural station.

Radio

The ABC – Australian Broadcasting Corporation – owns and produces most stations and programmes alongside numerous AM band radio stations. There are over 20 languages on multicultural stations and some city stations also focus on those who are disabled. The FM band has an assortment of worldwide mainstream, rock, ABC and community radios.

LANGUAGE

English is the official language of Australia. However, as

the population is ethnically diverse, a large number of community languages are spoken as well. In total there are about 140 different languages, including those spoken by established and long-settled Greek, Italian and Chinese communities. Recent arrivals are the Vietnamese, Russian and Portuguese, communities that are growing rapidly. Unfortunately, it is now extremely rare to hear any of the native Aboriginal languages.

Whatever your first language, English is necessary for communication in daily activities. Education and business dealings are conducted in English. There is an abundance of English courses available. The Department of Immigration and Multicultural and Indigenous Affairs, tertiary institutes like TAFE – Tertiary and Further Education – and privately-run English schools offer courses for every requirement. Some courses are run during the day and others are available after business hours.

'Down under' slang: useful words and phrases

ace – excellent or good	jumbuck – sheep
arvo – afternoon	mate – friend
Aussie – Australian	no worries ⎫ no problem,
boomer – a large male	she'll be right ⎭ I can do it
kangaroo	Pommy – someone from the
chewie – chewing gum	UK
cobber – friend	prezzy – present or gift
dag – funny person, or	ripper – fantastic or great
nerd	roo – kangaroo
earbashing – nagging	sprung – caught doing
fairdinkum – true or genuine	something wrong
galah – fool	tucker – food
g'day – hello	ute – utility vehicle or pickup
give it a burl – have a go	truck
hoon – hooligan	yabber – talk a lot
joey – baby kangaroo	yakka – work

RELIGION

In the 1950s, tensions between the dominant Roman Catholic and Protestant Churches promoted a puritanical, prejudiced society which showed up in the language, (migrants were referred to as dagos or wogs), censorship, and the fact that, although legal, divorce was difficult to obtain and frowned upon. Today, religion in Australia's diverse community is relatively issue-free. In this secular country, church attendances are amongst the lowest in the world. Every village, town and city has a Catholic and Anglican Church. United Churches are common and mosques and temples are mainly located in the major cities.

UTILITIES

Electricity

Electricity in Australia is very dependable and supplied at 220 – 240 volts, throughout the entire country. Outlets for 110 volt shavers are found in most hotels and motels. You will need a converter and a special flat three-pinned adaptor for other appliances such as hairdryers. The best place to buy adaptors is at the airport in your home country as you are leaving.

Water

Water supplied to all towns and cities within Australia is clean and tap water is safe to drink. Bottled mineral water is also available everywhere.

TIME AND PUBLIC HOLIDAYS

Australia has three time zones for most of the year:

◆ Eastern Standard Time – Queensland, Canberra, New South Wales, Victoria and Tasmania – is ten hours ahead of Greenwich Mean Time.

- Central Australian Time – South Australia and Northern Territory – is nine and a half hours ahead.

- Western Standard Time – Western Australia – is eight hours ahead.

During summer this pattern changes with daylight saving:

- Western Australia and Queensland do not have daylight saving.

- The other States start and finish it at different times.

The national holidays are:

New Year's Day (1 January)	Queen's Birthday (second
Australia Day (26 January)	Monday in June, except for
Good Friday	Western Australia where it
Easter Saturday	is the last weekend in
Easter Monday	September)
Anzac Day (25 April)	Christmas Day (25 December)
	Boxing Day (26 December)

Each State also has an additional public holiday of its own. All banks, post offices, private offices, government and shops are closed on national holidays.

WEATHER

Australia is situated in the Southern Hemisphere, which means that the seasons are the reverse of Europe and North America:

- December to February – summer
- March to May – autumn
- June to August – winter
- September to November – spring.

Since fine, mild weather occurs during all seasons, any time is suitable to visit most areas of Australia. The following is a guide as some months are warmer and drier than others. In central Australia summer is generally too hot for comfort.

Northern Territory and Queensland (The sunshine states)
The far north of these two territories has a very tropical climate. November/December to March/April is when the 'wet', or more commonly known by the locals, as the 'green season' occurs. The best time to visit the unique Great Barrier Reef and the north is from May to October when the climate is near perfect.

Tasmania
Tasmania is far south, so summer (December to May) is the best time to enjoy this beautiful island.

South Australia
Spring and autumn are the ideal travelling periods within these Territories.

Western Australia
The moderate and enjoyable temperatures of spring (September to November) and a profusion of wild flowers, make this the best time to visit.

Victoria and NSW
Victoria is notorious for its changeable and unpredictable weather. Be prepared for cold winds, rain and searing heat in one day. Sydney's summers, with the desert on one side and the sea on the other, are usually very hot and humid but the beaches are plentiful!

Winter

Winter in Australia can be similar to Europe depending on where you live. In Melbourne, the seasons can vary within a day, so a jacket, scarf and umbrella are required, but be prepared to remove them when the rain passes. Further north up the coast, the temperature hardly changes. In summer, shorts and tee shirt are worn and in winter, light trousers and a sweatshirt.

Australia also has three major alpine and ski resorts located in Victoria. Mount Buller is a popular family resort, while prominent cross-country ski areas are found at Lake Mountain and Mount Stirling. The snow season starts in June, on Queen's Birthday weekend, and usually finishes in the first week of October.

For more information contact: *www.mtbuller.com.au*

TELEPHONE SYSTEM

Australia has an excellent public telephone service with phones available in the usual locations. Most phones accept cash but you can buy phone cards from kiosks, convenience stores, post offices and newsagents in A$5, A$10 and A$20 denominations.

A local call costs 40 cents for unlimited time. Subscriber Trunk Dialling (STD) for calling long distance is available on most public and private phones. Dial the regional code (02 Sydney, 03 Melbourne) followed by the local number. These calls are usually cheapest after 7pm and before 8am. Telstra, Optus and AAPT offer competitive rates. Toll free numbers are common for many business numbers. Numbers beginning with 1800 are usually toll-free, but not always. 0800 numbers are free calling.

Numbers beginning with 13 are charged at a rate higher than a local call. Often these numbers may be applicable to a specific state or STD district only. Numbers beginning with 014, 015, 018, 019, 040, 041 or 042 are mobile or car phones.

Calling Australia: Remember to check country time differences; also between states.

To call from UK or South Africa dial 00 61 then area code then local number.

To call from USA or Canada dial 0 1161 then area code then local number.

Directory information: dial as above then 12455 (charge-able).

Emergency calls for fire, police and ambulance services can be made by dialling 000 anywhere in Australia – this is a 24-hour number.

WHAT TO WEAR

Dress codes tend to reflect the relaxed Australian lifestyle and neat casual clothes are acceptable at most restaurants and night-clubs. Business activities require a suit and tie except for in the very far north where the weather is so hot that shorts and open neck shirts are acceptable and comfortable.

HEALTHCARE FOR VISITORS

◆ United Kingdom residents who are travelling in Australia are entitled to free public hospital treatment. Proof of UK identity and residency is required, either your passport or your NHS medical card and as well, your temporary entry permit.

◆ Overseas travellers should be aware that they may not be covered by the free Government Medicare system for ambulance travel, dental treatment, visits to the doctor and prescriptions. You will need to enrol at a local Medicare office if you require medical services. You can do this after your treatment. Some charges may be refunded and you will have to claim them at the local office before you leave the country. Comprehensive travel and health insurance is therefore strongly recommended, as the bills can be high.

The telephone directory lists public hospitals, dentists, after-hours medical and pharmaceutical services as well as the Poisons Information Service.

Pharmacies or chemists

Pharmacies or chemists are qualified to dispense advice and sell prescribed medication, general medication, cosmetics and toiletries. Late-night chemists are available in the city centres. A roster system is usually worked in the small towns and suburbs so at least one pharmacy will be open for a few hours over the weekend.

SAFETY RULES FOR OUTSIDE

◆ *Swim only* in areas patrolled by lifesavers and between the flags.

- Make sure someone is always with you when fishing or swimming. Beware of sharks.

- On *total fire ban* days open fires and barbecues are not permitted.

- Australia has *several poisonous snakes and spiders, but the only other dangerous animals are the crocodiles* in the far north. Danger zones for these reptiles are well signposted.

The Australian sun is very strong, especially in the middle of summer. It is very easy to be badly burnt and suffer from heat stroke. Always wear sunscreen lotion and a hat, and avoid sunbathing in the middle of the day. Dress to protect your skin on sunny days. This is especially important for young children. Most schools insist on caps and a good sunscreen, and will encourage children to protect themselves.

DISCOVERING AUSTRALIA

Fly-drive holidays are the best way to discover Australia. Purchase a good travel guide and start with the city that you fly into, then head north. An itinerary of 2–3 days to one week is suggested for the drive from Sydney to Brisbane with stopovers as required. Then fly to the Great Barrier Reef for a relaxing and different experience.

The standard of accommodation throughout Australia is high and ranges from the five star standard (A$500 +) per night, (Sydney's hotels are the most expensive) to backpackers' hostels. Private farm accommodation is another option.

Learn to dive over four to six days in Cairns's warm, tropical waters off the Great Barrier Reef. Contact: *info@divers-den.com www.divers-den.com*

Travel overland off the beaten track and experience the outback in a 4WD vehicle. Tours start from Sydney, Cairns, Darwin, Uluru, or Adelaide and range in length from 13 to 75 days. Other tours covering the Northern Territory are five days long. A mixture of camping, hostels and farm stays gives an authentic taste of the 'Aussie experience'.

Contact: *www.jarmbie.com.au* or email: *info@jarmbie. com.au* or *www.australian-outlook.co.uk* or email: *info@-wayoutback.com.au*

Specialist holidays and outdoor activities include the following. *Bushwalking* in the state-managed national parks. Some exceptional walks are Cradle Mountain in Tasmania, the McDonnell Ranges in the Northern Territory and the Blue Mountains in New South Wales. For more information look under 'National Parks' in the government listings at the front of the telephone directory. *Aboriginal Heritage Tours* give the traveller a chance to experience the remarkable landscape from an Aboriginal perspective as their spirituality is closely connected to the land. The visitor may be taken to remote areas, Arnhem Land or Kakadu National Park in the Northern Territories, which are normally open only to Aborigines. Camel-trekking is available as a one-hour jaunt or a two-week trek and most of the popular tours start at Alice Springs. *Ecotourism* is a fast-growing tourist industry which offers opportunities to stay at Eco-lodges, watch the diverse wildlife and visit remote wilderness areas. Contact *www.ecotourism.org.au*

Student and youth travel

In order to be eligible for discounts on travel and admission to attractions, you must be able to provide an International Student Identity Card. As Australia has a widespread network of youth hostels and backpacker hostels, young visitors are advised to join the International Youth Hostels Federation before leaving their home country. Hostels may provide free board and accommodation in return for work. Homestay with an Australian family is a popular option. Check out: *www.studyabroadlinks.com.search/australia/homestay_ programs* or *www.craigslist.com*

Camping

All Australian campsites are inexpensive and accept tents, campervans and caravans. The amenities are normally clean and well kept. The only exception to this would be the National Parks where the campsite may simply be an area set aside for bush camping. Most campsites also have on-site vans available for rent, which is a cheaper alternative to a hotel or motel. Coastal sites are very special as they are usually beside a beach. National Park offices are located in each State and offer advice, information and maps. The best place to hire or buy campervans and or holiday equipment is in the *Yellow Pages* and these can be found at Information Offices or at your hotel or motel.

Entry to attractions

Annual membership of the National Trust will give you free entry into Australia's historic buildings. In Sydney it is advisable to purchase a Sydney Pass, which covers harbour cruises, ferries and bus services.

Touring by car

If you decide to explore Australia by car, remember that cities and towns generally have long distances between them, but the major highways are well signed and of a high standard. Make sure you always take plenty of water with you. Most people choose to fly between the major cities and rent a car for that area. For extended touring, it may be worthwhile buying a car or campervan. Most cars have air-conditioning. Membership of the Automobile Association (each State has its own) entitles you to a free breakdown service, and maps and other useful literature are available. The Automobile Association can be contacted at: 216 Northbourne Avenue, Canberra ACT 2601. Tel: (from overseas) +61 2 6247 7311. Email: *aaa@aaa.asn.au*

A suggested three- to five-week itinerary is to drive starting from Melbourne and head north up the coast to Sydney. Stop for a cruise on the Murray River and then on to Brisbane and the Gold Coast. It is suggested that you fly to Cairns and hire a car there to explore one of the world's oldest rainforests.

Sailing

Sail your own yacht around the 74 safe and very beautiful Whitsunday Islands for five or more days. You can drop the anchor and swim or dive the coral reef, fish for dinner and enjoy the peace and tranquillity of the protected bays and inlets. Yachts vary in size from 28 ft to 47 ft, can accommodate from two to 12 people and there is a choice of over 55 vessels. *www.boatingO2.com.au, www.australian charters.com.au, www.australianaccom.com/boatcharters. asp*

Travelling by train

Another alternative is to travel around New South Wales by train with unlimited stopovers over a set time at a reasonable cost. Backpacker Rail passes range from A$218 for 14 days to A$273 for 30 days. The East Coast Discovery pass covers set routes (A$300–400) and lasts six months. These passes can only be purchased by non-Australians in their homeland. Phone agents: UK 870 751 5000, Canada 416 322 1034, US 1 310 643 0044/420.

Disabled visitors

Australians are very aware of the requirements of disabled people. Most new buildings have wheelchair access and some rental cars have hand controls. The Australian Tourist Commission can provide a fact sheet, *Travel in Australia for people with disabilities.* Also contact Nican for a directory of accommodation and facilities. Advance notice is best when booking accommodation, any form of travel, museums or galleries, cinemas, restaurants, taxis and rental cars. When travelling on interstate trains, be careful to check the corridor widths as some may be too narrow for a wheelchair.

Useful Contacts

The most up-to-date information regarding migration to Australia can be found at the Australian Government website, *www.immi.gov.au.*

DIAC OFFICES
Below are details of all DIAC offices outside Australia, where immigration applications are processed, relevant information is available and visas are issued to successful applicants.

Country	Internet/email/fax
Albania – Tirana	*www.greece.embassy.gov.au*
Argentina – Buenos Aires	*www.argentina.embassy.gov.au/*
Austria – Vienna	*dima-vienna@dfat.gov.au*
Bangladesh – Dhaka	*dima-dhaka@dfat.gov.au*
Belgium – Brussels	*www.belgium.embassy.gov.au/*

Bosnia-Herzegovina –
  Sarajevo   *www.vienna.mission.gov.au*
Brazil – Brasilia   *dima-brasilia@dfat.gov.au*
Brunei Darussalam –
  Bandar Seri Begawan   *dima-brunei@dfat.gov.au*
Bulgaria – Sofia   *www.greece.embassy.gov.au*
Burma (renamed Myanmar)
  – Rangoon   *dima-rangoon@dfat.gov.au*
Cambodia – Phnom Penh   *dima-phnom.penh@dfat.gov.au*
Canada – Ottawa   *www.canada.embassy.gov.au*
Chile – Santiago   *dima-santiago@dfat.gov.au*
Croatia – Zagreb   *www.croatia.embassy.gov.au*
Cyprus – Nicosia   *dima.nicosia@dfat.gov.au*
Egypt – Cairo   *dima-cairo@dfat.gov.au*
Federate Republic of
  Micronesia – Pohnpei
Fiji – Suva   *dima-suva@dfat.gov.au*
France – Paris   *www.france.embassy.gov.au*
Germany – Berlin   *www.germany.embassy.gov.au/*
Greece – Athens   *dima-athens@dfat.gov.au*
Hungary – Budapest   *dima-budapest@dfat.gov.au*
India – New Delhi   *dima-newdelhi@dfat.gov.au*
Indonesia – Jakarta   *dima-bali@dfat.gov.au*
Iran – Tehran   *dima-tehran@dfat.gov.au*
Ireland – Dublin   *dima-dublin@dfat.gov.au*
Israel – Tel Aviv   *dima-tel.aviv@dfat.gov.au*
Italy – Rome   *dima-rome@dfat.gov.au*
Japan – Tokyo   *dima-tokyo@dfat.gov.au*
Jordan – Amman   *www.jordan.embassy.gov.au/*
Kenya – Nairobi   *dima-nairobi@dfat.gov.au*
Kiribati – Tarawa   *dima-tarawa@dfat.gov.au*
Korea – Seoul   *dima-seoul@dfat.gov.au*
Laos – Vientiane   *dima-vientiane@dfat.gov.au*
Lebanon – Beirut   *dima-beirut@dfat.gov.au*
Macedonia – Skopje   *www.serbia.embassy.gov.au*
Malaysia – Kuala Lumpur   *www.malaysia.embassy.gov.au/*
Malta – Malta   *dima-malta@dfat.gov.au*
Mauritius – Port Louis   *dima-port.louis@dfat.gov.au*
Mexico – Mexico City   *dima-mexico.city@dfat.gov.au*

Montenegro – Podgorica	*www.serbia.embassy.gov.au*
Netherlands – The Hague	*dima-the.hague@dfat.gov.au*
New Caledonia – Noumea	*dima-noumea@dfat.gov.au*
New Zealand – Auckland	*dima-auckland@dfat.gov.au*
Nigeria – Lagos	*dima-lagos@dfat.gov.au*
Pakistan – Islamabad	*dima-islamabad@dfat.gov.au*
Papua New Guinea – Port Moresby	*dima-port.moresby@dfat.gov.au*
Peoples Republic of China	
– Beijing	*www.china.embassy.gov.au/*
– Hong Kong	*www.hongkong.china.embassy.gov.au/*
– Shanghai	*www.shanghai.china.embassy.gov.au/*
Philippines – Manila	*dima-manila@dfat.gov.au*
Poland – Warsaw	*dima-warsaw@dfat.gov.au*
Portugal – Lisbon	*www.portugal.embassy.gov.au/*
Romania – Bucharest	*www.serbia.embassy.gov.au*
Russia – Moscow	*www.russia.embassy.gov.au/*
Samoa – Apia	*dima-apia@dfat.gov.au*
Serbia – Belgrade	*www.serbia.embassy.gov.au*
Singapore – Singapore	*dima-singapore@dfat.gov.au*
Slovakia	*www.vienna.mission.gov.au*
Slovenia – Ljubljana	*www.vienna.mission.gov.au*
Solomon Islands – Honiara	*dima-honiara@dfat.gov.au*
South Africa – Pretoria	*www.southafrica.embassy.gov.au/*
Spain – Madrid	*dima-madrid@dfat.gov.au*
Sri Lanka – Colombo	*dima-colombo@dfat.gov.au*
Taiwan – Taipei	*dima-taipei@dfat.gov.au*
Thailand – Bangkok	*dima-bangkok@dfat.gov.au*
Timor (East)	*dima-dili@dfat.gov.au*
Tonga – Nuku'alofa	*dima-nuku'alofa@dfat.gov.au*
Turkey – Ankara	*dima-ankara@dfat.gov.au*
– Istanbul	*dima-ankara@dfat.gov.au*
United Arab Emirates – Dubai	Fax: 9714 331 4729
United Kingdom – London	*www.uk.embassy.gov.au/*
United States – Washington	*www.usa.embassy.gov.au/*
– Los Angeles	*dima-los.angeles@dfat.gov.au*
Vanuatu – Port Villa	*dima-port.vila@dfat.gov.au*

Vietnam – Ho Chi Minh
   City   *www.hcmc.vietnam.embassy.*
                                 gov.au/
          – Hanoi   *www.vietnam.embassy.gov.au/*
Zimbabwe – Harare   *dima-harare@dfat.gov.au*

GETTING HELP WITHIN AUSTRALIA

If you have travelled to Australia and need information once you have arrived then the DIAC World Index has contact details for places within Australia.

Australia Migration Offices

Queensland
Brisbane, Cairns, Southport and Thursday Island

South Australia
Adelaide

Western Australian
Perth

Tasmania
Hobart

New South Wales
Parramatta, Rockdale, The Rocks and On Shore Protection

Victoria
Melbourne, City Centre, Dandedong and Preston

Northern Territory
Darwin

Australian Capital Territory
ACT Regional Office and Central Office

ENGLISH LANGUAGE TESTS

Should you be requested to undergo an English Language
Test the following addresses will be useful:

Country	Contact details
Albania	*elsona@icc.al,eu.org*
Algeria	Fax: 2230067
Angola	Fax: 2333331
Argentina	Fax: 13117747
Australia	*pullyng@janus.cqd.edu.au*
Austria	*exams@bc-vienna.at*
Bahrain	Fax: 241272
Bangladesh	*DTO@The BritishCouncil.net*
Belarus	Fax: 172364047
Belgium	Fax: 22270841
Bosnia	Fax: 00387 71 200890
Brazil	Fax: 41 224 1024
Brunei	Fax: 2453221
Bulgaria	Fax: 92 9434425
Burma	*MayWin.Than@bc*
Cambodia	*palum.idpcam@bigpond.com.kh*
Cameroon	Fax: 215691
Canada	Fax: 519 7483505
Chile	Fax: 56 2 2361199
China	*bc.guangzhou@bc-guangzhou. sprint.com*
Colombia	Fax: 12187754
Costa Rica	*instbrit@sol.racsa.co.cr*
Croatia	Fax: 385 1424888
Cyprus	*bcexams.nicosia@britcoun.org.cy*
Czech Republic	*lucie.koranova@britcoun.cz/ ivana.machajova@britcoun.cz*
Denmark	Fax: 33321501
Eastern Adriatic	*Dejana.Vukajlovic@britcoun.org.yu*
Ecuador	*dl@gye.satnet.net*
Egypt	*hala.eid@-alexandria.sprint.com*
Eritrea	Fax: 11127230
Ethiopia	Fax: 1552544
Fiji	*aidw@is.com.fj*

Finland	Fax: 9629626
France	*margaret.dalrymple@bc-paris.* *bcouncil.org*
Germany	*elfie.konrad@britcoun.de*
Ghana	Fax: 21663337
Great Britain	Fax: 0207 815 1608
Greece	Fax: 31 282498 or 13 634769
Hong Kong	*www.education.com.hk/idp*
Hungary	Fax: 13425728
India	Fax: 448523234 or 222852024
Indonesia	*fcargill@indosat.net.id*
Iran	*mam@sinasoft.net*
Ireland	*ALC@ucd.ie* or Fax: 00 353 21 903 223
Israel	Fax: 2283021 or 35221229
Italy	Fax: 0039064814296 or 0039 064814296
Jamaica	Fax: 001876 9297090
Japan	*edaust@gol.com*
Jordan	Fax: 6656413
Kazakhstan	Fax: 3272633339
Kenya	Fax: 2339854
Korea	Fax: 82514425435 or 8227738063
Kuwait	Fax: 2520069
Lao PDR	*vtcollege@laonet.net*
Latvia	Fax: 7830031
Lebanon	Fax: 1864534
Lithuania	*monika@bc-vilnius.ot.it*
Madagascar	Fax: 226690
Malaysia	*info@johorbahru.idp.edu.au*
Mali	Fax: 2222214
Malta	*admin@chamber-commerce.org.mt*
Mauritius	Fax: 4549553
Mexico	*marilu.groenwold@bc-mexico.* *bcouncil.org*
Mongolia	Fax: 761358659
Morocco	*britcoun.morocco.bcmor.org.ma*
Mozambique	Fax: 1421577
Namibia	Fax: 61227530

Nepal	Fax: 1224076
Netherlands	Fax: 206264962
New Zealand	*monasterioj@rimul.chchp.ac.nz*

Other offices in: Palmerston North, Auckland, Dunedin, Hamilton and Wellington

Nigeria	Fax: 422 501 58
Norway	Fax: 51534856
Oman	Fax: 212508 or 699163
Pakistan	*aeo@khi.compol.com*
Panama	Fax: 230730
Paraguay	Fax: 21203871
Peru	*postmaster@bc-lima.org.pe*
Philippines	Fax: 63 2 815 9875
Poland	Fax: 26219955
Portugal	Fax: 315 2 208 3068
Qatar	Fax: 423315
Romania	Fax 40 1210 0310
Russia	*bc.moscow@bc-moscow.sprint.com*
Saudi Arabia	Fax: 38268753 or 26726341
Senegal	Fax: 221 821 8136
Singapore	*info@singapore.idp.edu.au*
Slovakia	Fax: 7 533 47 05
Slovenia	*info@britishcouncil.si*
South Africa	Fax: 313057335 or 021 462 3960
Spain	Fax: 44762016 or 71172552
Sri Lanka	Fax: 1587079
Sudan	Fax: 11774935
Sweden	Fax: 8344192
Switzerland	Fax: 31 3011459
Syria	Fax: 963 11 332 1467
Taiwan	*info@taipei.idp.edu.au*
Thailand	*austcent@loxinfo.co.th*
Tunisia	Fax: 1353985
Turkey	Fax: 2122527474
Ukraine	Fax: 0442945507
United Arab Emirates	Fax: 2664340
Uruguay	Fax: 2921387
Venezuela	Fax: 58 2 952 9691
Vietnam	Fax: 84 8 846 5573

Yemen   Fax: 1244120
Zimbabwe   Fax: 4737877

Other offices
Britain

England	Harrogate	**Northern Ireland**
Bath	Leeds	Belfast
Birmingham	Liverpool	
Bournemouth	Manchester	**Scotland**
Brighton	Norwich	Aberdeen
Bristol	Nottingham	Edinburgh
Canterbury	Oxford	Glasgow
Colchester	Plymouth	
Coventry	Portsmouth	**Wales**
Cambridge	Southampton	Aberystwyth
Durham	York	Cardiff
Exeter		Swansea

There are also IELTS centres in the following locations. You will be able to locate these addresses on *www.immi.gov.au*

Armidale	Darwin	Southport
Adelaide	Hobart	Sydney
Brisbane	Melbourne	Townsville
Cairns	Newcastle	Wagga Wagga
Canberra	Perth	Wollongong

QUICK REFERENCE WEB ADDRESSES

Australian Government	*www.australia.gov.au*
Business Entry Point	*www.business.gov.au*
How to Register a	*www.asic.gov.au/info4companies/*
Company etc (ASIC)	*index.html*
Bureau of Statistics	*www.abs.gov.au*
Tax Office	*www.ato.gov.au*
Tax reform (GST)	*www.taxreform.ato.gov.au*
Medicare	*www.medicareaustralia.gov.au*
Industry (incl	
Industry profiles)	*www.ausindustry.gov.au*

Trade Commission	*www.austrade.gov.au*
Customs Services	*www.customs.gov.au*
Australian Info Industrial Association	*www.aiia.com.au*
Institute of Engineers	*www.engineersaustralia.org.au*
CSIRO (including industrial information sheets)	*www.csiro.com*
Dept of Industry Science and Resources	*www.disr.gov.au*
Invest Australia	*www.investaustralia.gov.au*
Intellectual Property, patents, trademarks and design	*www.ipaustralia.gov.au*
ABC – news & weather	*www.abc.net.au/news/weather/ default.htm*
The Australian – news and weather	*www.news.com.au*
Australian *White Pages*	*www.whitepages.com.au*
Australian *Yellow Pages*	*www.yellowpages.com.au*

Appendix 1

Skilled Occupations List

Managerial and administration

Occupation	ASCO Code	Points
Childcare Co-ordinator	1295-11	60
Company Secretary	1212-11	50
Construction Project Manager	1191-11	50
Director of Nursing	1292-11	60
Education Managers (not elsewhere classified)	1293-79	50
Engineering Manager	1221-11	60
Environment, Parks and Land Care Manager	1299-17	50
Finance Manager	1211-11	60
General Manager	1112-11	60
Human Resource Manager	1213-11	60
Information Technology Manager	1224-11	60
Laboratory Manager	1299-13	50
Medical Administrator	1292-13	50
Policy and Planning Manager	1291-11	50
Production Manager (Manufacturing)	1222-11	50
Production Manager (Mining)	1222-13	50
Project Builder	1191-13	50
Regional Education Manager	1293-15	50
Research and Development Manager	1299-11	50
Sales and Marketing Manager	1231-11	60
Sports Administrator	1299-19	50
Supply and Distribution Manager	1223-11	60
Welfare Centre Manager	1299-15	50

Professionals and tradespersons

Occupation	ASCO Code	Points
Aboriginal and Torres Strait Islander Health Worker	3493-11	40
Accountant – Corporate Treasurer	2213-11	60
Accountant – External Auditor	2212-11	60
Accountant	2211-11	60

Accountant – Internal Auditor	2212-13	50
Actuary	2293-15	50
Acupuncturist	2394-13	50
Advertising Specialist	2221-17	50
Agricultural Adviser	2114-21	50
Agricultural Scientist	2114-19	50
Aircraft Maintenance Engineer (Avionics)	4114-15	60
Aircraft Maintenance Engineer (Mechanical)	4114-11	60
Aircraft Maintenance Engineer (Structures)	4114-13	60
Aircraft Maintenance Engineers Supervisor	4114-01	60
Ambulance Officer	3491-11	40
Anatomist or Physiologist	2113-11	50
Apparel Cutter	4941-17	60
Architect	2121-11	60
Architectural Associate	3121-13	40
Archivist	2299-15	50
Art Teacher	2491-11	50
Audiologist	2399-11	50
Automotive Electrician	4212-11	60
Baker	4512-11	60
Binder and Finisher	4913-11	60
Biochemist	2113-17	50
Biomedical Engineering Associate	3129-11	40
Blacksmith	4123-11	60
Boat Builder and Repairer	4981-13	60
Botanist	2113-13	50
Branch Accountant	3211-11	40
Bricklayer	4414-11	60
Broadcast Transmitter Operator	4992-17	60
Building Associate Professionals (not elsewhere classified)	3129-79	40
Building Associate	3121-11	40
Building Inspector	3121-17	40
Building Surveyor	2549-79	50
Business and Information Professionals (not elsewhere classified)	2299-79	50
Business Machine Mechanic	4315-13	60
Butcher	4511-11	60
Buttermaker or Cheesemaker	4519-13	60
Cabinetmaker	4922-11	60
Cable Jointer	4313-13	60
Canvas Goods Maker	4944-13	60
Careers Counsellor	2513-17	50
Carpenter	4411-13	60

Carpenter and Joiner	4411-11	60
Cartographer	2123-11	50
Chef – Head Chef	3322-01	60
Chef	3322-11	60
Chemist	2111-11	50
Chemistry Technical Officer	3112-11	40
Chiropractor	2387-11	60
Civil Engineering Associate	3122-11	40
Civil Engineering Technician	3122-13	40
Commodities Trader	3212-17	40
Communications Linesperson	4316-13	60
Community Worker	2512-13	50
Computing Professionals – Applications and Analyst Programmer	2231-17	60
Computing Professionals – Computer Systems Auditor	2231-21	60
Computing Professionals – Software Designer	2231-15	60
Computing Professionals – Systems Designer	2231-13	60
Computing Professionals – Systems Manager	2213-11	60
Computing Professionals – Systems Programmer	2231-19	60
Computing Professionals (not elsewhere classified)	2231-79	60
Computing Support Technician	3294-11	40
Confectioner	4519-15	60
Conservator	2549-11	50
Cook	4513-11	60
Copywriter	2534-19	50
Counsellors (not elsewhere classified)	2513-79	50
Dance Teacher	2491-15	50
Dental Hygienist	3492-13	40
Dental Specialist	2381-13	60
Dental Technician	3492-15	60
Dental Therapist	3492-11	40
Dentist	2381-11	60
Dietitian	2393-11	60
Disabilities Services Officer	3421-17	40
Drainer	4431-15	60
Drama Teacher	2491-17	50
Dressmaker	4941-15	60
Drug and Alcohol Counsellor	2513-13	50
Economist	2522-11	50
Editor	2534-11	50
Electorate Officer	2549-13	50

Electrical Engineering Associate	3123-11	40
Electrical Engineering Technician	3123-13	40
Electrical Powerline Tradesperson	4313-11	60
Electrician (Special Class)	4311-13	60
Electronic Engineering Associate	3124-11	40
Electronic Engineering Technician	3124-13	40
Electronic Equipment Tradesperson	4315-11	60
Electronic Instrument Tradesperson (Special Class)	4314-13	60
Electroplater	4126-13	
Engineer – Aeronautical Engineer	2129-11	60
Engineer – Agricultural Engineer	2129-13	60
Engineer – Biomedical Engineer	2129-15	60
Engineer – Building and Engineering Professionals (not elsewhere classified)	2129-79	60
Engineer – Chemical Engineer	2129-17	60
Engineer – Civil Engineer	2124-11	60
Engineer – Civil Engineering Technologist	2128-11	60
Engineer – Electrical Engineer	2125-11	60
Engineer – Electrical or Electronics Engineering Technologist	2128-15	60
Engineer – Electronics Engineer	2125-13	60
Engineer – Engineering Technologists (not elsewhere classified)	2128-79	60
Engineer – Industrial Engineer	2129-19	60
Engineer – Materials Engineer	2127-15	60
Engineer – Mechanical Engineer	2126-11	60
Engineer – Mechanical Engineering Technologist	2128-13	60
Engineer – Mining Engineer	2127-11	60
Engineer – Naval Architect	2129-21	60
Engineer – Petroleum Engineer	2127-13	60
Engineer – Production or Plant Engineer	2126-13	60
Engineer Electronics Engineer	2125-13	60
Engineer Mechanical Engineering Technologist	2128-13	60
Engineer Petroleum Engineer	2127-13	60
Engineering Associate Professionals (not otherwise specified)	3129-79	40
Engraver	4115-21	60
Environmental Health Officer	2543-13	50
Environmental Research Scientist	2114-11	50
Extractive Metallurgist	2119-15	50
Family Counsellor	2513-15	50
Family Support Worker	3421-19	40
Farrier	4123-13	60

Fashion Designer	2533-11	50
Fibrous Plasterer	4412-11	60
Financial Dealers and Brokers (not elsewhere classified)	3212-79	40
Financial Institution Branch Manager	3211-13	40
Financial Investment Adviser	3213-11	40
Financial Market Dealer	3212-15	40
Fitter	4112-11	60
Flat Glass Tradesperson	4982-11	60
Floor Finisher	4423-11	60
Forester	2114-13	50
Furniture Finisher	4929-13	60
Furniture Upholsterer	4942-11	60
Futures Trader	3212-13	40
Gasfitter	4431-13	60
Gem Cutter and Polisher	4983-13	60
General Clothing Tradesperson	4941-11	60
General Communications Tradesperson	4316-11	60
General Electrician	4311-11	60
General Electronic Instrument Tradesperson	4314-11	60
General Fabrication Engineering Tradesperson	4121-11	60
General Gardener	4623-11	60
General Mechanical Engineering Tradesperson	4111-11	60
General Plumber	4431-11	60
Geologist	2112-11	50
Geophysicist	2112-13	50
Glass Blower	4982-13	60
Graphic Designer	2533-13	50
Graphic Pre-Press Tradesperson	4911-11	60
Greenkeeper	4622-11	60
Gunsmith	4115-19	60
Hairdresser	4931-11	60
Head Gardener	4623-01	60
Health Information Manager	2299-11	50
Historian	2529-11	50
Hotel or Motel Manager	3323-11	50
Hotel or Motel Manager (Diploma level)	3323-11	40
Illustrator	2533-19	50
Industrial Designer	2533-15	50
Industrial Relations Officer	2291-15	50
Insurance Broker	3212-19	40
Intelligence Officer	2299-19	50
Intensive Care Ambulance Paramedic	3491-13	40
Interior Decorator	3999-11	40

Interior Designer	2533-17	50
Interpreter	2529-13	60
Jeweller	4983-11	60
Joiner	4411-15	60
Journalists and Related Professionals (not elsewhere classified)	2534-79	50
Land economist	2295-13	50
Landscape Architect	2121-13	50
Landscape Gardener	4623-13	60
Leather Goods Maker	4944-11	60
Legal Practitioner Barrister	2521-11	60
Legal Practitioner Solicitor	2521-13	60
Librarian	2292-11	50
Library Technician	3997-11	40
Life Scientists	2113-79	50
Lift Mechanic	4311-15	60
Locksmith	4115-15	60
Management Consultant	2294-11	50
Marine Biologist	2113-19	50
Market Research Analyst	2221-15	50
Marketing Specialist	2221-13	50
Massage Therapist	3494-11	40
Master Fisher	2542-13	40
Materials Scientist	2119-19	50
Mathematician	2293-11	50
Mechanical Engineering Associate	3125-11	40
Mechanical Engineering Technician	3125-13	40
Mechanical Services and Air-conditioning Plumber	4431-19	60
Medical Grade Shoemaker	4943-13	60
Medical Laboratory Technical Officer	3111-11	40
Medical Practitioner – Anaesthetist	2312-11	60
Medical Practitioner – Dermatologist	2312-13	60
Medical Practitioner – Emergency Medicine Specialist	2312-15	60
Medical Practitioner – General Medical Practitioner	2311-11	60
Medical Practitioner – Obstetrician and Gynaecologist	2312-17	60
Medical Practitioner – Ophthalmologist	2312-19	60
Medical Practitioner – Paediatrician	2312-21	60
Medical Practitioner – Pathologist	2312-23	60
Medical Practitioner – Psychiatrist	2312-27	60
Medical Practitioner – Radiologist	2312-29	60

Medical Practitioner – Specialist Medical		
Practitioners (not otherwise specified)	2312-79	60
Medical Practitioner – Specialist Physician	2312-25	60
Medical Practitioner – Surgeon	2312-31	60
Medical Scientist	2115-11	60
Metal Casting Tradesperson	4125-11	60
Metal Fabricator	4122-11	60
Metal Machinist (First Class)	4112-13	60
Metal Polisher	4126-11	60
Metallurgical and Materials Technician	3129-13	40
Meteorologist	2119-13	50
Mine Deputy	3129-15	40
Motor Mechanic	4211-11	60
Museum or Art Gallery Technician	3999-13	40
Museum or Gallery Curator	2549-21	50
Music Teacher	2491-13	50
Natural and Physical Science Professionals		
(not elsewhere classified)	2119-79	50
Naturopath	2394-11	50
Nurse – Registered Developmental Disability		
Nurse	2326-11	60
Nurse – Registered Mental Health Nurse	2325-11	60
Nurse – Registered Midwife	2324-11	60
Nurse – Registered Nurse	2323-11	60
Nurseryperson	4621-11	60
Occupational Health and Safety Officer	2543-11	50
Occupational Therapist	2383-11	60
Oenologist	2549-17	50
Office Manager	3291-11	40
Optical Mechanic	4999-11	60
Optometrist	2384-11	60
Organisation and Methods Analyst	2294-13	50
Orthoptist	2399-13	50
Orthotist	2399-15	50
Osteopath	2387-13	60
Painter and Decorator	4421-11	60
Panel Beater	4213-11	60
Park Ranger	2114-15	50
Parole or Probation Officer	3421-11	40
Pastrycook	4512-13	60
Patents Examiner	2549-15	50
Patternmaker-Grader (Clothing)	4941-19	60
Personnel Consultant	2291-13	50

Personnel Officer	2291-11	50
Pharmacist – Industrial Pharmacist	2382-13	50
Pharmacist – Retail Pharmacist	2382-15	60
Pharmacist Hospital Pharmacist	2382-11	60
Physical Metallurgist	2119-17	50
Physicist	2119-11	50
Physiotherapist	2385-11	60
Piano Tuner	4999-17	60
Picture Framer	4929-11	60
Plumbing Engineering Associate	3121-21	40
Plumbing Inspector	3121-19	40
Podiatrist	2388-11	60
Policy Analyst	2299-17	50
Precision Instrument Maker and Repairer	4115-11	60
Pressure Welder	4122-13	60
Primary Products Inspector	3991-11	40
Print Journalist	2534-13	50
Printing Machinist	4912-11	60
Project or Program Administrator	3292-11	40
Property Manager	3293-13	40
Psychologist – Clinical Psychologist	2514-11	60
Psychologist – Educational Psychologist	2514-13	60
Psychologist – Organisational Psychologist	2514-15	60
Psychologist – Psychologists (not elsewhere classified)	2514-79	60
Public Relations Officer	2221-11	50
Quality Assurance Manager	2294-15	50
Quantity Surveyor	2122-11	60
Radio Journalist	2534-17	50
Radiographer – Medical Diagnostic Radiographer	2391-11	60
Radiographer – Nuclear Medicine Technologist	2391-15	60
Radiographer – Radiation Therapist	2391-13	60
Radiographer Sonographer	2391-17	60
Real Estate Agency Manager	3293-11	40
Real Estate Salesperson	3293-15	40
Records Manager	2299-13	50
Recreation Officer	2549-19	50
Refrigeration and Air-conditioning Mechanic	4312-11	60
Rehabilitation Counsellor	2513-11	50
Residential Care Officer	3421-15	40
Roof Plumber	4431-17	60
Roof Slater and Tiler	4413-11	60
Safety Inspector	3992-11	40

Sail Maker	4944-15	60
Sales Representative	2222-11	50
Sales Representative	2222-13	50
Sales Representative	2222-15	50
Saw Maker and Repairer	4115-17	60
Screen Printer	4914-11	60
Seafarer – Ship's Engineer	2542-15	40
Seafarer – Ship's Master	2542-11	40
Seafarer – Ship's Officer	2542-19	40
Seafarer – Ship's Surveyor	2542-17	40
Sheetmetal Worker (First Class)	4124-11	60
Shipwright	4981-11	60
Shoemaker	4943-11	60
Signwriter	4422-11	60
Small Offset Printer	4912-13	60
Smallgoods Maker	4511-13	60
Social Professionals (not elsewhere classified)	2529-79	50
Social Worker	2511-11	60
Soil Scientist	2114-17	50
Solid Plasterer	4415-11	60
Speech Pathologist	2386-11	60
Statistician	2293-13	50
Stockbroking Dealer	3212-11	40
Stonemason	4416-13	60
Supervisor, Aircraft Maintenance Engineers	4114-01	60
Supervisor, Automotive Electricians	4212-01	60
Supervisor, Bakers and Pastrycooks	4512-01	60
Supervisor, Bricklayers	4414-01	60
Supervisor, Cabinetmakers	4922-01	60
Supervisor, Carpentry and Joinery Tradespersons	4411-01	60
Supervisor, Communications Tradespersons	4316-01	60
Supervisor, Electrical Distribution Tradespersons	4313-01	60
Supervisor, Electricians	4311-01	60
Supervisor, Electronic and Office Equipment Tradepersons	4315-01	60
Supervisor, Electronic Instrument Tradespersons	4314-01	60
Supervisor, Fibrous Plasterers	4412-01	60
Supervisor, Floor Finishers	4423-01	60
Supervisor, Forging Tradespersons	4123-01	60
Supervisor, General Fabrication Engineering Tradespersons	4121-01	60
Supervisor, General Mechanical Engineering		

Tradespersons	4111-01	60
Supervisor, Hairdressers	4931-01	60
Supervisor, Meat Tradespersons	4511-01	60
Supervisor, Metal Casting Tradespersons	4125-01	60
Supervisor, Metal Finishing Tradespersons	4126-01	60
Supervisor, Metal Fitters and Machinists	4112-01	60
Supervisor, Motor Mechanics	4211-01	60
Supervisor, Painters and Decorators	4421-01	60
Supervisor, Panel Beaters	4213-01	60
Supervisor, Plumbers	4431-01	60
Supervisor, Precision Metal Tradespersons	4115-01	60
Supervisor, Refrigeration and Air-conditioning Mechanics	4321-01	60
Supervisor, Roof Slaters and Tilers	4413-01	60
Supervisor, Sheetmetal Tradespersons	4124-01	60
Supervisor, Signwriters	4422-01	60
Supervisor, Solid Plasterers	4415-01	60
Supervisor, Structural Steel and Welding Tradespersons	4122-01	60
Supervisor, Toolmakers	4113-01	60
Supervisor, Vehicle Body Makers	4215-01	60
Supervisor, Vehicle Painters	4214-01	60
Supervisor, Vehicle Trimmers	4216-01	60
Supervisor, Wall and Floor Tilers and Stonemasons	4416-01	60
Surveying and Cartographic Associate	3121-15	40
Surveyor	2123-13	60
Tailor	4941-13	60
Teacher – Education Officer	2493-11	50
Teacher – Pre-Primary School Teacher	2411-11	60
Teacher – Primary School Teacher	2412-11	60
Teacher – Secondary School Teacher	2413-11	60
Teacher – Vocational Education Teacher (trades)	2422-11	60
Teacher – Vocational Education Teacher (non-trades)	2422-11	50
Technical Sales Representatives	2222-79	50
Technical Writer	2534-21	50
Television Journalist	2534-15	50
Textile, Clothing or Footwear Mechanic	4112-15	60
Toolmaker	4113-11	60
Tradespersons and Related Officers		
Training Officer	2291-17	50
Translator	2529-15	60
Tree Surgeon	4623-15	60

Upholsterers and Bedding Tradespersons (not elsewhere classified)	4942-79	60
Urban and Regional Planner	2523-11	50
Valuer	2295-11	50
Vehicle Body Maker	4215-11	60
Vehicle Painter	4214-11	60
Vehicle Trimmer	4216-11	60
Veterinarian	2392-11	60
Wall and Floor Tiler	4416-11	60
Watch and Clock Maker and Repairer	4115-13	60
Welder (First Class)	4122-15	60
Welfare Worker	2512-11	60
Wood Tradespersons (not elsewhere classified)	4929-79	60
Wood Turner	4921-13	60
Youth Worker	3421-13	40
Zoologist	2113-15	50

In addition the following occupations may be nominated under the Employer Nomination Scheme but not the General Skilled Migration Categories.

Occupation	ASCO Code
Artistic Director	1296-13
Commissioned Defence Force Officer	1294-11
Commissioned Fire Officer	1294-13
Commissioned Police Officer	1294-15
Faculty Head	1932-13
Importer or Exporter	1192-11
Manufacturer	1193-11
Media Producer	1296-11
School Principal	1293-11
Specialist Managers (not elsewhere classified)	1299-79
Wholesaler	1192-13

Appendix 2

CONTACT DETAILS OF ASSESSING AUTHORITIES

AACA – Architects Accreditation Council of Australia Inc
Email: *registrar@acca.org.au*
Website: *www.aaca.org.au*
Fee payable: A$1050.00

AASW – Australian Association of Social Workers
Email: *aaswosea@aasw.asn.au*
Website: *www.aasw.asn.au*

ACS – Australian Computer Society
Email: *info@acs.org.au*
Website: *www.acs.org.au*
Fee payable: A$350.00/450.00

ADC – Australian Dental Council
Phone: 61 3 9415 1638
Website: *www.dentalcouncil.net.au*

AECOP – Australian Examining Council for Overseas Physiothera-
pists Inc
Email: *noosr@detya.gov.au*
Website: *www.physiocouncil.com.au/*
Fee payable: AS220.00

AIM – Australian Institute of Management
Email: *barbarak@aim.com.au*
Website: *www.aim.com.au*
Fee payable: A$300.00

AIMS – Australian Institute of Medical Scientists
Email: *aimsnat@medeserv.com.au*
Website: *www.aims.org.au*
Fee payable: A$300.00

AIQS – Australian Institute of Quantity Surveyors
Email: *AIQS@compuserve.com*
Website: *www.aiqs.com.au*

AIR – Australian Institute of Radiography
Email: *air@A-I-R.com.au*
Website: *www.A-I-R.com.au*

AIWCW – Australian Institute of Welfare and Community Workers
Email: *aiwcw@ozemail.com.au*
Website: *www.aiwcw.org.au/*

AMSA – Australian Maritime Safety Authority
Email: *maritime.qualifications@amsa.gov.au*
Website: www.amsa.gov.au
Fee payable: A$100.00

ANCI – Australian Nursing Council Incorporated
Email: *anci@anmc.org.au*
Website: *www.anmc.org.au/*

APC – Australasian Podiatry Council
Email: *apodc@ozemail.com.au*
Website: *www.apodc.com.au*
Fee payable: A$500.00

APEC – Australian Pharmacy Examining Council Incorporated
Email: *enquiries@pharmacyboard.sa.gov.au/*
Website: *www.pharmacyboard.sa.gov.au/*

APS – Australian Psychological Society
Email: *contactus@psychology.org.au/*
Website: *www.psychology.org.au/*

ASCPA – Australian Society of Certified Practising Accountants
Website: *www.cpaaustralia.com.au/*
Fee payable: A$300.00

CASA – Civil Aviation Safety Authority
Email: *fcl.licensing@casa.gov.au*
Website: *www.casa.gov.au*

DAA – Dieticians Association of Australian
Email: *nationaloffice@daa.asn.au/*
Website: *www.daa.asn.au/*

Engineers Australia
Website: *www.engineersaustralia.org.au/*

Fee payable: AS275.00

ICAA – Institute of Chartered Accountants of Australia
Website: *www.icaa.org.au*
Fee payable: A$300.00

ISA – Institute of Surveyors, Australia
Email: *isa@isaust.org.au*
Website: *www.isaust.org.au*
Fee payable: A$200.00

NAATI – National Accreditation Authority for Translators and
   Interpreters
Website: *www.naati.com.au*

NOOSR – National Office of Overseas Skills Recognition
Email: *educational.noosr@dest.gov.au/*
Website: *www.aei.dest.gov.au/*
Fee payable: A$360.00

OCANZ – Optometry Council of Australia and New Zealand
Email: *ocanz@ozemail.com.au*
Website: *www.ocanz.org/*

SPA – Speech Pathology Association of Australia
Website: *www.speechpathologyaustralia.org.au/*

TAA/TRA – Trades Assessing Authority/Trades Recognition Aus-
   tralia
Website: *www.migration.wa.gov.au*
Fee payable: A$390.00

Index

Going to Live in Brazil
ROMASA STOREY

Brazil, the sleeping giant of South America, awakes to welcome foreign investors to its country to join in the race of the 21st Century to see who will be the mightiest economy along with Russia, India and China (BRIC countries). Already, it is the world's largest ethanol producer and bio-energy superpower and is still rich in natural resources despite the plundering of the Portuguese Colonialists from 1500 onwards. Today Brazil offers the foreign investor political stability without any threat of terrorism or impending natural disasters and an opportunity to live the high life in one of the world's most delectable and romantic scenic settings.

ISBN 978-1-84528-310-0

Emigrating to New Zealand
STEVE HORRELL

'A must for anyone considering emigrating to NZ.' – *Amazon*

This book is an indispensable guide to the roller coaster ride that is the emigration process. It covers all the topics and issues that anyone thinking of emigrating to New Zealand will need to know about, from the discussion phase through to making friends when you're there.

ISBN 978-1-84528-116-8

How to Retire Abroad
ROGER JONES

'A "must read" for sun-seeking retirees.' – *Living for Retirement*

'Provides advice and hard facts on finding a location, getting there, and coping once you're there . . . packed with useful addresses and phone numbers.' – *The Mirror*

ISBN 978-1-85703-976-4

Getting into Australia
MATHEW COLLINS

'Easy to read and to dip in and out of, for that nuts and bolts information, this book is a must-have for all would-be migrants.' – *Australian News*

ISBN 978-1-84528-011-6

Getting into Canada
BENJAMIN KRANC & ELENA CONSTANTIN

'*Getting into Canada* is a clearly set out, highly practical guide on how to make a successful application for permanent or temporary residence in Canada. It is an invaluable companion to the migration process.' – *Canada News*

ISBN 978-1-85703-537-7

Getting a Job Abroad
ROGER JONES

'Don't even think about packing your suitcase until you've read this ... excellent source of information. Practical advice on finding the country where you can make the most of your skills.' – *The Guardian*

'Highly informative...lots of hard information and a first class reference section.' – *Outbound Newspapers*

ISBN 978-1-85703-418-9

Living & Working in India
KRIS RAO AND DR IAN BEADHAM

The purpose of this book to ease the transition between Western and Indian cultures, giving a wealth of advice in terms of language, culture, lifestyle, education, health, housing, working practices and regulations. It is will guide the foreign worker from before they leave their country to touchdown in India, adjusting to the language, customs and eating habits of their Indian friends and colleagues.

With this book in their travel bag, the reader can be confident that their visit to India will be an experience of a lifetime.

ISBN 978-1-84528-199-1

Living and Working in Hong Kong
RACHEL WRIGHT

'Wright's guide will more than pay for itself in time saved.' – *South China Morning Post*

This book gives flavourful descriptions of what to expect from life in Hong Kong. Each chapter includes up-to-date information and well-informed opinion and comment on social and professional issues. Interviews with a broad cross-section of the expatriate community in Hong Kong provide useful insights into life in Hong Kong and invest the book with the colour and authenticity of personal experience.

ISBN 978-1-84528-195-3

Living & Working in Australia
LAURA VELTMAN

'Chock full of advice and pointers for successful entry.'
– *The Guardian*

'An indispensable guide to your new life.' – *Australian Outlook*

ISBN 978-1-84528-183-0

A City by City Guide to Living and Working in Australia
ROBERTA DUMAN

'This is a knowledgeable, down to earth guide to life Down Under.'
– *A Place in the Sun*

'Provides comprehensive information about what to expect from each in terms of lifestyle, employment opportunities, recreation, residential options and information on education and childcare for those with families.' – *Birmingham Post*

ISBN 978-1-84528-089-5

Getting a Job in Australia
A step-by-step guide to finding work Down Under
NICK VANDOME

'An indispensable guide for anyone wishing to work in Australia
... delivering the latest information on tax reform, wage rates and
employment organisations, the latest on pensions, Newstart
allowances and economic conditions; useful web site addresses that
include on-line job searching outside Australia...' – *Australian
Outlook*

'Will appeal to would-be migrants across a wide range of business
backgrounds... a very useful guide.' – *Emigrate Magazine*

ISBN 978-1-85703-921-4

How To Books are available through all good bookshops, or you can order direct from us through Grantham Book Services.

Tel: +44 (0)1476 541080
Fax: +44 (0)1476 541061
Email: *orders@gbs.tbs-ltd.co.uk*

Or via our website

www.howtobooks.co.uk

To order via any of these methods please quote the title(s) of the book(s) and your credit card number together with its expiry date.

For further information about our books and catalogue, please contact:

How To Books
Spring Hill House
Spring Hill Road
Begbroke
Oxford
OX5 1RX

Visit our web site at

www.howtobooks.co.uk

Or you can contact us by email at info@howtobooks.co.uk